PARENTAL CONFLICT

Outcomes and interventions for children and families

Jenny Reynolds, Catherine Houlston,
Lester Coleman and Gordon Harold

First published in Great Britain in 2014 by

Policy Press
University of Bristol
6th Floor
Howard House
Queen's Avenue
Bristol BS8 1SD
UK
t: +44 (0)117 331 5020
f: +44 (0)117 331 5367
pp-info@bristol.ac.uk
www.policypress.co.uk

North America office:
Policy Press
c/o The University of Chicago Press
1427 East 60th Street
Chicago, IL 60637, USA
t: +1 773 702 7700
f: +1 773 702 9756
sales@press.uchicago.edu
www.press.uchicago.edu

© Policy Press 2014

British Library Cataloguing in Publication Data
A catalogue record for this book is available from the British Library

Library of Congress Cataloging-in-Publication Data
A catalog record for this book has been requested

ISBN 978 1 44731 581 0 paperback

The right of Jenny Reynolds, Catherine Houlston, Lester Coleman and
Gordon Harold to be identified as authors of this work has been asserted by them
in accordance with the Copyright, Designs and Patents Act 1988.

Cover design by Policy Press
Image kindly supplied by www.istock.com
Printed and bound in Great Britain by Hobbs, Southampton
Policy Press uses environmentally responsible print partners

CONTENTS

Contents

FOREWORD

All happy families resemble one another, but each unhappy family is unhappy in its own way. (*Anna Karenina*, Leo Tolstoy, part 1, chapter 1)

When I first saw Mark, he was 8 years old and had severe abdominal pains and headaches which had been troubling him for several weeks. His GP and his parents were both concerned that there was an underlying disease process. After a number of basic investigations, it was clear to me that his parents, whom he brought with him for the appointment, were clearly not getting along well and I could sense that this was the source of his distress, as I had done with so many other families I had seen over the years. Up until recently I have felt very much unprepared to deal with such cases.

Four out of 10 marriages end in divorce now compared with around a third in 1979. The circumstances are frequently conflictual and the children often suffer and come to the attention of various adults who care for them. Practitioners like myself, need to be aware of the different forms of parental conflict and how this affects children's health and wellbeing at different ages and stages of their lives and most importantly how we can support and signpost parents to appropriate help.

This authoritative resource reviews the evidence and skilfully takes the reader though the distinctions between 'constructive' and 'destructive' forms of parental conflict, its effects on sleep, immune system, hormonal systems, and emotional health of the child and the theoretical basis on which children process such conflict in their daily lives. We read how children react in different ways depending on their gender, age, temperament and genetic make-up as well as the effects of peers and others who interface with their lives. This review looks critically at the components of what works in parenting programmes, both universal and targeted, and the additional effectiveness of those which specifically address parental conflict in their design.

Most importantly, by the end one realises oneself that, with appropriate training, there is help which we can provide to families within our spheres of influence and high quality programmes which one can signpost parents to. I was particularly struck by the fact that we need these skills when we take a journey with parents through key transition points in the lifecourse of their child whether it be pregnancy and new parenthood or moving to school or dealing with separation or bereavement. OnePlusOne has succeeded in collating an impressive evidence base, which policy makers, programme designers and practitioners will find invaluable when dealing with unhappy families they come in contact with.

Professor Mitch Blair
Consultant Paediatrician and Officer for Health Promotion
Royal College of Paediatrics and Child Health, UK

PREFACE

According to a recent UK government report (Casey, 2012), families experience 'legacies of trouble' with serious problems passed on from one generation to the next. Specifically, children who experience early trauma such as parental abuse, maltreatment, poor parenting and high levels of inter-parental conflict and violence are at serious risk not only in terms of their own wellbeing, but also in relation to the perpetuation of these behaviours across generations. Rather than offer quick-fix solutions to addressing endemic family problems, the Casey report concludes what scientific evidence has emphasised for several decades: that if we are to address the needs of children in families, we must look beyond trying to fix single problems in the short term, to addressing multiple causes and multiple outcomes associated with harsh family experiences that cause families and the individuals that comprise them significant difficulties in the short and long term. We must also recognise that remediating these problems such that improvements or positive changes in the quality of life that individuals experience takes time.

With this objective in mind, there cannot be a more important task across the complementary fields of child development research, social work and clinical practice, health and education, intervention development and family policy than the promotion of knowledge and public understanding as to what promotes healthy child development and positive family functioning – as it is recognised that healthy families are the bedrock of a healthy society.

What makes or breaks a healthy family? Many factors contribute to addressing this question of significant social, clinical and policy relevance. One of the strongest predictors of how a family functions however relates to how adults in any given family experienced family life as children. Specifically, the economic and cultural circumstances, levels of parental support and parenting experiences, the compositional type of family (e.g. cohabiting, married, single, divorced, remarried), attributes of parental mental health and the quality of relations between parents/caregivers serve as strong predictors of healthy child development and long-term wellbeing. By understanding how these factors affect children in the short and long term, we are better positioned to understand how we may help troubled families, endorse and help sustain well-functioning families and ultimately remediate the significant personal, economic and societal costs of broken families and the individuals that comprise them.

This book serves to review evidence relating to family influences on children with the objective of informing what helps and what hurts children in the context of family life marked by disrupted family relationships. Specifically, how the inter-parental relationship, and in particular high levels of inter-parental conflict and discord, serves as a significant influence on children's development. Rather than suggest that this feature of family life serves as a single cause of negative outcomes for children however, the book reviews evidence to suggest that the quality of the inter-parental relationship serves as a starting place to understand the constellation of wider family influences on children. Understanding the role of this component of family life on developmental outcomes for children is required reading for anybody working with children and families where conflict between couples is a factor in children's lives (e.g. parental separation-divorce, child maltreatment). Indeed, the bottom-line objective of this book is to review and translate state-of-the-art evidence highlighting the role of the couple relationship as an influence on children's development, with recommendations provided for practitioners and policy makers aimed at promoting positive outcomes for children, parents and families in the UK where everyday family life is marked by high levels of inter-parental conflict and discord.

As a pioneer in the promotion of healthy couple relationships and an ambassador for the development and implementation of evidence-led practice and policy, OnePlusOne is to be commended for conducting this timely review of evidence. Given present government interest and recognition of the importance of early family experiences on long-term individual development, it is hoped that this book will serve as a primer for those interested in understanding how to improve the lives of children today – thereby promoting improved outcomes for the parents, families and children of tomorrow!

Gordon Harold
Andrew and Virginia Rudd Professor of Psychology
University of Sussex, UK

CHAPTER 1

CONFLICT IN CONTEXT

There is growing interest and recognition regarding the importance of couple relationships and how they can influence child wellbeing. A large body of evidence exists which documents the significance of parental relationships on children's social, emotional, cognitive, behavioural and physical development. Inter-parental conflict (conflict between a child's parents) is one area which appears to have considerable impact on child outcomes.

It is not simply the presence of conflict per se which affects outcomes for children, but rather the characteristics of this conflict and how parents deal with it that seems to matter most. Conflict is particularly destructive to children when it is frequent, unresolved, intense, or about the child (Cummings and Davies, 2010). This book reviews the latest evidence showing how children who experience high levels of destructive conflict between their parents are at serious risk not only in terms of their own wellbeing, but also in relation to the perpetuation of these behaviours later in life.

This book focuses on recent research, over the last 10 years and provides an insight into the outcomes for children of exposure to destructive conflict as well as how children are affected, and why some children appear more vulnerable than others. In other words, there is more of an understanding of 'why, when, and how' parental conflict affects some but not all children. Specifically, reviewed research into the physiological and neurobiological impacts, in addition to the intergenerational transmission of conflict, are particularly innovative additions.

Another key area of emerging evidence is in relation to conflict interventions delivered to couples and parents. Evidence suggests that involving couples in intervention activities and focusing on elements of the couple relationship is more effective than those which deal solely on improving parenting (Cowan et al., 2011). A variety of programmes, with different approaches in terms of content and goals, are outlined. What unites the interventions covered in this publication is a shared emphasis on the importance of working with couples, whether they are together or separated, with a focus placed on early intervention. The evidence is assessed to identify what aspects of these interventions appear to be most effective, and areas for future research are highlighted.

A review of what works in conflict interventions is important in addressing key messages for policy makers, practitioners and researchers. As examples, those who work directly with families from a wide range of sectors (including health practitioners such as midwives and health visitors, to children centre workers and teachers), are well placed to identify parents at risk or struggling with conflict and will thus benefit from the evidence outlined in this book. Front-line workers who, over time, build a relationship of trust with families are well placed in the identification, signposting and delivery of conflict interventions. Knowing what matters about conflict, why and what can be done about it are crucial for practitioners working in this field. The evidence in this review can help in designing new training and intervention programmes to help these frontline workers work more effectively with families in conflict.

Within this context, the aim of this book is to collate and summarise the research evidence to increase understanding of how and why children can be affected by conflict between their parents and what can be done to help support families experiencing such conflict. This publication is designed to be accessible for health practitioners and other front-line workers who engage closely with families and children. The scope of this review is also of interest to policy makers, commissioners of health and social care services, students of social sciences and those with a general interest in public health, families and relationships.

In more detail, the book begins by providing some context to current family relationships, in which parental conflict is explored, before identifying different types of conflict (Chapter 2); considering the impact of inter-parental conflict on children (Chapter 3); how inter-parental conflict affects children (Chapter 4); and why some children are affected more than others (Chapter 5). The later chapters of the book cover a review of conflict-based interventions for couples (Chapter 6); and what this evidence suggests about how to help families (Chapter 7). The final chapter presents a 'call to practice' by concluding the evidence and presenting recommendations for those involved in the lives and wellbeing of children, as well as identifying emerging areas of interest and future research needed to better support families in conflict (Chapter 8).

Changing family life

This first chapter introduces readers to the notion of parental conflict. The topic is contextualised within a climate of changing family forms, and a refocus towards relationship quality rather than relationship status; the importance of managing conflict; and an understanding that conflict between parents affects children.

Family life has changed considerably over the past forty years: Fewer people are getting married, with 241,100 marriages in England and Wales, recorded in 2010 compared with 404,737 in 1971 (ONS, 2013a). Divorce rates have remained stable, but these reflect the overall proportion of the population who experience divorce and disguise the fact that a greater proportion of marriages end in divorce now compared with the 1970s (Lloyd and Lacey, 2012). In fact, the latest estimates are that 42% of marriages will end in divorce (ONS, 2012), increasing from around a third in 1979.

At the same time, cohabitation has become more common. Survey evidence shows that the proportion of non-married women aged 18 to 49 who were cohabiting increased from one in ten (11%) in 1979 to one third (34%) in 2011 (Office for National Statistics, 2013b). Also, around eight in ten of those marrying for the first time in 2004–07 lived together beforehand, up from three in ten in 1980–84 (Beaujouan and Bhrolcháin, 2011). Although it is more difficult to obtain reliable data around cohabitation it appears that rates of separation are even higher amongst cohabiting rather than married parents. For example, analysis of census data found that 82% of married couples surveyed in 1991 were still together in 2001 compared with 61% of couples who were cohabiting in 1991 (Wilson and Stuchbury, 2010).

Whether couples are married or cohabiting, or living apart in a long-term relationship, children are affected when relationships break down (Coleman and Glenn, 2009). For example, in 2009, just under half of divorcing couples had at least one child under sixteen, 21% of these children were under five, 63% were under eleven (Office for National Statistics, 2012). Looking at non-married couples, cohabiting couples who were together at the birth of their child were five times more likely to split up before the child turned three and three times more likely to split up by the time the child turned five than married couples (Goodman and Greaves, 2010).

In the light of significant changes in family structure and concerns regarding the implications for children, there can be a tendency amongst politicians, policy makers and researchers to focus on family structure, i.e. whether parents are married, cohabiting or parenting alone, in addressing family-level influences on children. However, being in a relationship does not always confer being in a satisfying relationship. In studying relationship quality and blood pressure, Holt-Lunstad and colleagues (2008) conclude that 'one is better off single than unhappily married' (p. 5). Indeed, recent research findings have demonstrated that the effect of couple relationship quality on child behavioural outcomes is the same for children from different family formations (Garriga and Kiernan, Forthcoming).

In conjunction, further evidence, points to the significance of what goes on within the parental relationship, rather than the structure of the relationship between parents per se, as a primary factor underpinning the welfare of children. This reflects the fact that while divorce as an event is stressful for children, experiencing the process of parental separation and divorce may be even more stressful. For example, most children take around two years to adjust to divorce and may experience physical, emotional or behavioural difficulties over that period (Hetherington and Stanley-Hagen, 1999). Some children, however, experience difficulties long before and long after their parents' divorce (Harold and Murch, 2005), while a proportion of children do better, with improved psychological outcomes after parental divorce (Amato, 2005) (see Coleman and Glenn, 2009 for a comprehensive review conducted for OnePlusOne).

There are a number of factors affecting children's adjustment following divorce or separation such as multiple family transitions (how frequently a parent re-partners), paternal mental health, and adjustment to new step-parents and step-siblings (Coleman and Glenn, 2009). However, inter-parental conflict is one of the main factors that explains why some children fare more poorly than others during parental separation (Amato and Keith, 1991). Indeed, conflict between parents that is frequent, intense, child related, and unresolved may pose a significant risk for children irrespective of their parents' marital status (Harold and Murch, 2005). It can also play a part regardless of whether parents stay together or separate. Conflict between parents does not necessarily cease following parental separation and children may find themselves caught in the middle. Conflict can also remain a problem even if parents form a new relationship. Research on children's wellbeing in separated families and stepfamilies suggests that, while the level of conflict within these new families may be no higher than in first families, the greater number of relationships in which children are involved can serve to increase their overall exposure to parental conflict and its potentially damaging impact (Harold et al., 2001).

This book will outline the nature and mechanisms by which conflict can impact on children. It will also explore ways in which conflict can be managed by reviewing the evidence from a number of innovative conflict management interventions that have emerged over the last decade. At the outset, it should also be recognised that the array of influences on child outcomes in addition to conflict (such as stress, parenting, poverty and social circumstances) will not be outlined here. Also, the impact of relationship breakdown, unless this includes evidence on inter-parental conflict, is beyond the scope of this review. Readers are referred to the work by Luster and Okagaki (2006) for additional family influences on child outcomes, and reviews by Coleman and Glenn (2009) and Mooney et al (2009) on the consequences of relationship breakdown for children.

Introducing inter-parental conflict

Conflict in the context of personal and family relationships, including between parents, is a necessary and relatively 'normal' part of life (Harold and Leve, 2012). So when does conflict between parents become troubling for children? A recent survey found that, on average, some couples argue twice a week and arguments are followed by around two hours of withdrawn silence (OnePoll, 2009). That means many couples spend nearly 10 days a year not talking to each other. This is the closest research comes to providing statistics on conflict. As we will see in Chapter 2, the various types of conflict, ranging from passing comments to more overt aggressive behaviour, make calculations over the prevalence of conflict most difficult.

Some researchers have found that conflict between partners at one point in a relationship can predict happiness later on in the relationship when conflict is managed productively (Fincham and Beach, 1999). On the other hand, conflict is associated with relationship distress, physical and mental ill health, as well as divorce (Clements et al., 2004). What matters it seems, is how conflict is handled and whether couples can ensure that the negative ways of relating with one another associated with conflict do not outweigh positive ways of relating, such as being warm and affectionate (Driver et al., 2003). For example, in their long-term study of changes in marital satisfaction over time, Bradbury and Karney (2004) found that couples who possess poor communication and problem solving skills do not become dissatisfied with their relationship any quicker than couples who do possess those skills. What distinguished happier couples was what Bradbury and Karney described as a 'teflon coating' of positive emotionality. That is to say, couples who related to each other with warmth, affection and humour (positive emotionality) even during disagreements, somehow protected themselves from the potentially damaging impact of their poor problem solving and communication skills.

Without that emotional warmth, behaviours like the 'silent treatment', withdrawing, and failing to resolve arguments can be particularly destructive to relationships and increase the likelihood of relationship breakdown (Birditt et al., 2010). Other damaging behaviours include verbal and physical hostility and aggression, and reacting with scorn and contempt. Not only do these ways of dealing with conflict put the relationship at risk, as the research outlined in this publication demonstrates, they are also destructive for the children who witness them (Goeke-Morey et al., 2003). These contrasting types of conflict will be outlined in greater depth in Chapter 2.

Introducing child impacts

Interviews with, and surveys of, children show just how troubled they can be by an unhappy home (National Family and Parenting Institute, 2000; Smart et al., 2001; The Children's Society, 2009). Take the findings of a recent survey of young people by The Children's Society (2009): Young people who felt that their family got along well together had higher levels of wellbeing than children who felt their families did not. Whereas family structure (i.e. whether parents were married, separated, or cohabiting), explained just 2% of differences in children's wellbeing; how well the family got on explained 20% of the difference between children who rated themselves happy with life compared to those who did not.

Children's accounts are equally compelling and demonstrate how children are upset by parents' rows, often feeling caught in the middle, compelled to intervene, and haunted by what they have seen, as in the case of this seven year old:

> 'Everything I see and hear, it just goes inside my head, it's just like a prison in my head, it just shows me pictures and it's like a stereo going round and round, seeing all the things what they said when I was little...' (from Dunn and Deater-Deckard, 2001)

Or as this 16 year old described:

> 'When he married [stepmother], it made the whole arguments more heated really. I don't talk to either of my parents about either of them because arguments start and a lot of it gets directed at me, even though it's not really anything to do with me ... they are still arguing with each other through me, which isn't easy or nice.' (from Dunn and Deater-Deckard, 2001)

What are the consequences of this distress? A large body of evidence demonstrates that, for some children, their distress in the face of parental conflict translates into long-term psychological difficulties, including emotional and behavioural problems, difficulties settling and performing at school, problems with peers and others, trouble sleeping and other health related outcomes (Rhoades, 2008; Cummings and Davies, 2010; Mannering et al., 2011). These outcomes for children will be presented in greater depth in Chapter 3, and the mechanisms on how inter-parental conflict affects children will be outlined in Chapter 4.

Introducing why outcomes from inter-parental conflict differ for children

Not all children react the same. Much of the research conducted since OnePlusOne's first publication on couple conflict and children's wellbeing ten years ago (Harold et al., 2001) has tried to explain why some children are more likely to experience negative outcomes than others when exposed to 'risk' factors such as parental conflict. To address this question researchers have adopted a 'process-oriented' perspective in order to identify the particular mechanisms, sometimes referred to as mediating and moderating factors, that underlie differences in how children respond to risk factors such as inter-parental conflict. A moderating factor is one that influences the strength of relationship between conflict and child outcomes, whilst a mediating factor is one that helps to explain the relationship between the exposure to conflict and child outcomes.

This type of understanding means that we are better able to explain not only what happens when children are exposed to conflict, but 'why, when and how' children respond in different ways to instances of inter-parental conflict. Identifying the mechanisms that explain why some children experience serious difficulties in the context of inter-parental conflict, while other children seem relatively unaffected (i.e. resilient), enables us to develop more effective support targeted at children and families most vulnerable and at risk. These differing reactions to conflict will be presented in Chapter 5.

This opening chapter has introduced readers to the forthcoming content, partly by outlining what will, and what will not, be detailed in greater depth. For this and subsequent chapters, a summary of key points serves to distill the main points:

To summarise

- Conflict between parents, rather than the event of parental separation or divorce, is a key factor in explaining why some children fare better than others when parental relationships breakdown.
- Conflict is particularly detrimental to children, whether parents are together or apart, when it is frequent, unresolved, intense, or about the child.
- Couples who continue to hold on to more positive ways of relating in the midst of heated conflicts, and who can find ways to resolve an argument, are less vulnerable to relationship breakdown and their children are less at risk of developing emotional or behavioural difficulties.
- Research over the last decade has provided deeper insight into not only the outcomes for children of exposure to destructive conflict but also how children are affected and why some children appear more vulnerable than others. In other words, there is more of an understanding of 'why, when, and how' parental conflict affects some but not all children.

CHAPTER 2

UNDERSTANDING DIFFERENT TYPES OF CONFLICT

For many children conflict between parents is a natural and normal part of family life and does not signify the demise of the parents' relationship or any serious threat to wellbeing. For other children, however, conflict between parents is a serious source of stress with debilitating implications for their emotional and behavioural development (Harold and Leve, 2012). What constitutes differences in children's adaptation to inter-parental conflict?

How this conflict is handled is of primary importance when explaining child outcomes. Important aspects are the intensity of the conflict, the negativity expressed, or emotional tone, the behaviours parents adopt towards one another, the topic of conflict, and if and how things are resolved. Indeed, Lavner and Bradbury (2012) note the importance of negative communication having the capacity to erode relationships and lead to divorce, even among 'satisfied newly-weds'. This recent study emphasises the point that conflict and negative communication is a matter of great influence on the stability and quality of couple relationships, and one worthy of investment through intervention programmes, such as those reviewed in Chapter 6. The paper concludes:

'Thus it may only be several years into marriage – when additional stress emerges, or when fundamental disagreements about life values boil over – that negative communication exerts its impact...the present findings reaffirm the value of targeting negative communication in preventive interventions.' (from Lavner and Bradbury, 2012, p 8).

What type of conflict matters?

One important aspect of conflict is how often parents argue. Rather than getting used to conflict, children become more sensitive or reactive to it as they experience more of it (Erath and Bierman, 2006). In addition to the detrimental effects of frequent conflict, the content of conflict is also important in explaining effects on children. How parents argue, what they argue about, whether or not conflicts are about the child, and the extent to which conflict is resolved all influence whether or not children are adversely affected by conflict. Earlier work on children and inter-parental conflict distinguished between destructive, constructive and productive conflict suggesting that conflict could be productive when children learn from observing parents handle disagreements well. More recently, researchers have focused on the distinction between constructive and destructive conflict, rather than productive conflict (Goeke-Morey et al., 2003).

Differentiating destructive and constructive conflict

Destructive conflict

Conflict has been categorised as destructive or constructive according to how children react to it and how those reactions link to their long-term adjustment (Goeke-Morey et al., 2003; Cummings and Davies, 2010). Moreover, conflict is seen as constructive when it involves behaviours such as calm discussion and problem-solving support in the context of otherwise destructive conflict behaviours as children are significantly less distressed when conflicts are expressed calmly and resolved constructively (Cummings et al., 2003). Destructive conflict involves behaviours that evoke negative reactions in children, and is typically characterised by the following primary features.

Physical aggression

Children are particularly troubled by physical violence between parents and this behaviour is most strongly linked to adjustment problems (Cummings et al., 2000; Kitzmann et al., 2003). Evidence from laboratory studies and community samples highlight children's distress at observing physically aggressive conflicts (Cummings et al., 1989; Laumakis et al., 1998; Katz and Windecker-Nelson, 2006). Children are also more likely to get involved when conflicts involve physical aggression (Jouriles and Norwood, 1995). Getting involved in parents' conflict can put children at risk of physical abuse as well as psychological distress (Gerard et al., 2005; Franck and Buehler, 2007).

Verbal hostility

Children are also upset by verbal hostility, such as shouting, threats, and raised voices. When parents are verbally aggressive towards one another children may become scared, angry or sad and, over time, these reactions have been linked with psychological adjustment problems (Davies et al., 2002).

The silent treatment or nonverbal conflict

Children are as troubled by sulky conflicts, where parents give each other 'the silent treatment', as they are by overtly angry exchanges (Kerig, 1996; Katz and Gottman, 1997; Katz and Woodin, 2002). Note that this sulking behaviour is different to parents taking time-out to calm down and to consider how to resolve conflict (this applies to all references to 'silent treatment' in this book).

Despite parents' best endeavours, children are also aware of 'covert' conflict and its impact can be as damaging as more overt disputes (Bradford and Barber, 2008; Ablow and Measelle, 2009). One reason is that sulky, silent behaviour suggests to children that the disagreement will not get sorted out (Cummings et al., 1991) and children are left worrying about what that means for the stability of the family. In addition, children are also more likely to blame themselves for their parents' difficulties when parents are caught up in covert conflict, leaving them more vulnerable to internalising problems such as anxiety and depression (Ablow and Measelle, 2009).

Intense conflicts

Unsurprisingly, intense or heated arguments are generally more disturbing for children than milder disputes (Grych and Fincham, 1993). However, it is important to distinguish between conflicts that are merely expressive or emotional because of the character of each spouse and their relationship, and between arguments that are wrought with feelings of contempt, scorn or criticism.

Threats to family stability and intactness

Children are also upset by conflict that they perceive as a threat to family stability, specifically where conflict, according to a child's appraisal, threatens the intactness of the family (Laumakis et al., 1998).

When one partner withdraws

Children are particularly concerned when parents withdraw or walk away from an argument (Katz and Gottman, 1997). Indeed, one study found that withdrawal was more strongly linked to problems for children than marital conflict itself (Cox et al., 1997). Research demonstrates a link between withdrawal during conflict and parent's emotional unavailability to their children, particularly for fathers (Sturge-Apple et al., 2006). Research also shows that relationships in which one partner tends to withdraw are more vulnerable to serious problems or marital breakdown (Bradbury and Karney, 2004). It is possible that children are troubled by parental withdrawal because they are sensitive to the seriousness of marital problems and concerned that parents may separate (Cummings and Davies, 2002; Cummings and Davies, 2010).

Conflicts about children

Conflict is particularly distressing for children when they, or issues relevant to them, are the subject of dispute (e.g. Davies et al., 2002; Goeke-Morey et al., 2003; Jenkins et al., 2005; Shelton and Harold, 2007). For example, diary studies found conflicts about child-related themes heightened the likelihood of child aggression in the home (Cummings et al., 2004). One reason child-related conflicts are more harmful is that children may be more likely to get involved because they feel responsible for, and ashamed about, what is going on (Grych and Fincham, 1993; Shelton and Harold, 2007).

What about domestic violence?

Despite the availability of a considerable amount of research into the respective areas of spousal violence and child maltreatment, researchers have only recently begun to study the effects of domestic violence on children (Rivett et al., 2006). Most research in this area, however, has been directed toward identifying child outcomes associated with living in a violent home rather than on the processes that explain why some children appear resilient to the trauma associated with exposure to domestic violence while others go on to develop long-term, clinically significant emotional and behavioural problems (Sternberg et al., 1993; Holden et al., 1998). Might the effects of domestic violence on children be explained by (1) changes in the quality of relations children experience with their parent(s) as a result of the occurrence of violent exchanges between adults, and/or (2) the effects of violence on children's feelings of threat, self-blame, emotional insecurity and representations of family relationships in the context of violence? Does exposure to domestic violence constitute a qualitatively distinct dimension of family or parent discord, thereby overriding the processes that have been identified in explaining the effects of inter-parental conflict on children? If so, what does this mean for the development of future intervention programmes? These are questions that require further research attention and that are beyond the scope of the present review. Readers are referred to the work of Rivett et al (2006) where the impacts of domestic and other forms of physical violence on children are outlined in greater depth.

Constructive conflict

How it all ends

How conflicts are resolved and how parents relate to each other following the end of a conflict are also important factors in distinguishing between constructive and destructive conflict. For example, if a conflict is completely resolved it may counteract the negative impact of exposure to conflict (Cummings et al., 1989; Cummings et al., 1991; Goeke-Morey et al., 2007). However, the way in which the episode of conflict ends and the impact of this may also be more nuanced. For example, children react positively to compromise, but, submission, topic change and apology are seen as partial resolutions by children, although they are better than no resolution. The feelings underlying resolution are also important. If parents apologise with warm feelings, children see this as constructive (Goeke-Morey et al., 2007). However, apologies are destructive where they are accompanied by negativity and lack of warmth, in which case children see through the action to the underlying feelings.

What happens after a fight is also important. If children are aware that things have been resolved 'behind closed doors' from the warmth and tone of parents' ensuing conversations they are less troubled (Cummings and Wilson, 1999). The same is true if children are told that things have been sorted out. However, one study suggests that this is not the case for children from families experiencing significant discord. In fact, Winter et al. (2006) found that in troubled families, a mother's reassurance that differences have been resolved actually increased the risk posed by marital conflict. One reason may be that when the message does not fit the situation at hand or children's previous similar experiences (e.g., Lerner, 1983), or when the verbal communication does not correspond to the emotional message or atmosphere, children may actually become more sensitised to the situation and thus, feel more threatened and insecure (e.g., Morton et al., 2003).

Can conflict be constructive?

Conflict that is resolved is one feature of conflict between parents that can be described as constructive. Conflict is also described as constructive when parents continue to relate to one another in more positive ways, even when they disagree (Goeke-Morey et al., 2003). When parents use warmth and affection (Cummings et al., 2002), engage in problem-solving and offer one another support, even in the context of other more negative behaviours, children are less likely to see conflict as a threat (Goeke-Morey et al., 2003).

An on-going question in the literature is whether children can learn positive lessons from observing conflict between parents that is handled constructively. Relatively limited research has been conducted in this area. However, research suggests that children can actually benefit from observing constructive conflict by employing lessons learnt in their own social relationships (e.g. peers, siblings; Cummings et al., 2004) One recent study found that after taking account of young children's initial ability to get on well with others, one year later, those children exposed to constructive conflict showed more pro-social behaviour. For example they were more likely to use reasoning, problem-solving skills and resolve differences with peers than those exposed to destructive conflict (McCoy et al., 2009). There is emerging evidence, therefore, that children can learn helpful ways of relating from observing their parents' disagreements when parents handle those well, although more research is needed to consolidate this finding.

To summarise

- Children can develop difficulties when conflict between parents is handled destructively.
- Destructive conflict includes behaving in a way that is physically or verbally aggressive; sulking or the 'silent treatment'; getting caught up in highly intense or heated arguments; and withdrawing or walking away from an argument.
- Children are particularly upset when they, or issues relevant to them, are the subject of an argument.
- Children react more positively when parents can continue to relate to each other with warmth and positive regard in the midst of other more destructive ways of relating.
- Children may also be less troubled by conflict when parents are able to resolve an argument. This 'resolution' needs to be genuine, however; children are not fooled when parents tell them things have been sorted out but fail to relate to each

other in ways that demonstrate that the relationship has been repaired; parents' actions need to echo their words.
- There is emerging evidence that children can learn behaviours that are helpful in their relationships with others from observing parents handling conflict well. However, further research is required to confirm and expand our understanding of this.

CHAPTER 3

THE IMPACT OF INTER-PARENTAL CONFLICT ON CHILDREN

There exists a long standing and wide ranging body of evidence, going back over 30 years, documenting children's reactions to parental conflict (for reviews see Cummings and Davies, 1994; Grych and Fincham, 2001). This includes evidence collected using experimental, longitudinal, and naturalistic approaches to data collection, as children watch recordings of adults arguing or give their reactions to different scenarios) under carefully controlled experimental conditions (e.g. Davies et al., 2006). It also includes data from interviews with, or questionnaires completed by, parents, children and teachers (Cummings et al., 2002; Cummings et al., 2003). This involves children, parents and families being followed for long periods of time (longitudinal studies; see Harold and Conger, 1997), or other innovative means of obtaining children's views, such as using puppets (Ablow and Measelle, 2009), as well as diary accounts and observational studies (Crockenberg et al., 2007).

Together the data demonstrate that, in general, children are highly sensitive to parental conflict and their distress is apparent from an early age; as early as six months old according to some studies (Cummings and Davies, 1994; Harold et al., 2004; Crockenberg et al., 2007; Moore, 2010). Children's distress is apparent in facial expressions, gestures and actions indicating fear and anxiety, in biological regulatory processes i.e. how the body and brain respond to stressful situations (Van Goozen et al., 2007; Davies et al., 2008; El-Sheikh and Erath, 2011), and in their own accounts where children talk about being angry, sad, frightened or responsible (Smart et al., 2000; Dunn and Deater-Deckard, 2001). Children may also have different emotional responses to conflict depending on the nature of the dispute. For example, one study found children react to escalating and unresolved conflict with fear, while escalating conflicts about child-rearing provoke anger and sadness (Koss et al., 2011). This chapter looks at how these immediate responses translate into long-term difficulties for children who are exposed to destructive conflict between parents.

Emotional regulation: externalising and internalising problems

Two of the most well-established and most common outcomes for children are internalising (emotional) and externalising (behavioural) problems respectively (Cummings and Davies, 1994; Grych and Fincham, 2001). Over the last decade research has built on this large body of work and sought to identify the mechanisms underlying the link between inter-parental conflict and children's internalising and externalising symptoms respectively (see Davies et al., 2002; Davies et al., 2004; El-Sheikh et al., 2008).

Common behavioural difficulties, or externalising problems, in children associated with conflict include:

aggression, hostility, anti-social and non-compliant behaviour, delinquency and vandalism (Erath and Bierman 2006). Emotional problems, or internalising difficulties, associated with inter-parental conflict include depression, anxiety, withdrawal and dysphoria (Marks et al., 2001). Although early research suggested externalising problems were a more common outcome of exposure to inter-parental conflict (Fauber et al., 1990), recent research suggests that both internalising and externalising difficulties are a common response problem in children (Grych et al., 2003; Cummings et al., 2006).

Research indicates that children's repeated exposure to destructive inter-parental conflict can undermine children's capacity to regulate negative feelings of anger, sadness, or fear (Cummings and Davies., 2010; see Chapter 4 for details on the Emotional Security Perspective). This disrupted emotional regulation has been found to mediate the link between inter-parental conflict and children's internalizing and externalizing problems (Buehler, et al., 2007; Harold et al., 2004; Siffert and Schwarz, 2011).

Of course, inter-parental conflict is one of a number of factors associated with adverse family-based outcomes for children, including larger family size, disadvantaged socio-economic circumstances, poor parent–child relations and parental psychopathology, such as depression or substance abuse (Brooks-Gunn and Duncan, 1997; McMunn et al. 2001; Du Rocher Schudlich and Cummings, 2007; Harold et al., 2010). However, one of the main ways in which these factors are linked to poor emotional and behavioural outcomes is through their impact on family functioning (e.g. see Repetti et al., 2002). For example, evidence from multiple research perspectives collectively highlights that harsh economic circumstances affect partners' mental health and precipitates conflict between partners and between parent and child. At the same time, parents are likely to tend towards hostile, negative parenting, which, in turn, leads to the development of internalising and externalising symptoms in children (see review, McLoyd, 1998; Harold and Leve, 2012).

Family and social relationships

Not surprisingly, the impact of inter-parental conflict on children extends into other family and social relationships (Feldman et al., 2010). One way in which inter-parental conflict can impact on children's family relationships is through the quality of the father-child relationship and the level of father involvement. High conflict families are associated with lower father involvement (Kelly, 2000; Kari and Kay, 2005), and reduced father involvement is, in turn, associated with negative developmental outcomes for children and adolescents (Grych et al., 2004).

Children from high conflict homes are more likely to have poor interpersonal skills, problem-solving abilities and social competence (Du Rocher Schudlich et al., 2004a; Lindsey et al., 2006; Finger et al., 2010). A high conflict home is associated with parent–child conflict (Benson et al., 2008) as well as hostile relationships with siblings (Stocker and Youngblade, 1999) and conflict with peers in pre-school and school (Parke et al., 2001; Hipwell et al., 2005; Finger et al., 2010). For example, Finger et al. (2010) found a link between inter-parental conflict and young children's ability to get on with their peers in kindergarten in a sample of children followed from the age of one through to four years old.

Difficulties also extend into adolescence and adulthood, with research documenting difficulties in romantic relationships (Du Rocher Schudlich et al., 2004a; Kinsfogel and Grych, 2004). For example, Cui and Fincham (2010) found adolescents from high conflict homes were more likely to be involved in poor quality dating relationships marked by conflict.

One reason for problematic relationships is the impact of conflict on children's perceptions of themselves and their social worlds. Children from high conflict homes are more likely to perceive themselves and their social worlds more negatively and have more negative pictures or internal representations of family relationships (Du Rocher Schudlich et al., 2004a). Children then extend these negative representations to other people and settings (Grych et al., 2003; Schermerhorn et al., 2008). Consequently, children may be more withdrawn in social settings as they seek to avoid situations where they might get drawn into conflict (Gottman and Katz, 1989) or they may be more aggressive, because they perceive others as a threat (Bascoe et al., 2009). The growing body of research on biological regulatory processes (see Chapter 4) also points to differences in children's ability to regulate their responses to conflict in social situations (El-Sheikh et al., 2008; Laurent et al., in press)

Poor health

There is a well-documented link between relationship distress and breakdown and poor health outcomes for adults (Coleman and Glenn, 2009). Children's health is also at risk in the context of parental relationship difficulties (Troxel and Matthews, 2004; El-Sheikh et al., 2008). Conflict between parents is associated with: greater general health problems, chronic and acute health difficulties, digestive problems, fatigue (El-Sheikh et al., 2001), reduced physical growth (Montgomery et al., 1997), and headaches and abdominal pains (Stiles, 2002).

Research over the past decade has been unravelling the different physiological responses to inter-parental conflict and its impact on, and through, the body's systems, such as the body's flight and fight systems (e.g. autonomic nervous system) or hormonal mechanisms that manage the release of cortisol, adrenaline and other hormones (Katz, 2001; El-Sheikh et al., 2009). Over time the wear and tear on the body resulting from the burden placed on these systems leads to psychological distress and ill-health (Cummings and Davies, 2010). As outlined in Chapter 5, these psychophysiological systems also play a role in either buffering children from the impact of destructive conflict between parents or heightening their vulnerability (El-Sheikh et al., 2008; El-Sheikh and Erath, 2011).

Earlier research also points to links between family climate and behaviours risky to health, such as smoking and alcohol abuse and promiscuous sexual activity (Glendinning et al., 1997; Blum et al., 2000; Repetti et al., 2002). This partly reflects the impact of inter-parental conflict on the parent–child relationship and on consistent, attentive care-giving (Cox et al., 2001). It may also reflect young people's attempts to 'self-medicate' in order to manage the psychological distress arising out of their family environment (Repetti et al., 2002).

Sleep

Child sleep disturbances are believed to be a marker of the impact of family stress on neurobiological functioning (El-Sheikh et al., 2007) and problems that emerge during early childhood can often persist later in development

(Mannering et al., 2011). Sleep problems are also associated with difficulties at school (El-Sheikh et al., 2007a).

Recent research has identified a link between inter-parental conflict and sleep disturbances (El-Sheikh et al., 2006). For example, a study that assessed infants aged 9 months and then 18 months found relationship instability significantly predicted child sleep problems both concurrently and across time (Mannering et al., 2011). The link held even after taking account of relationship instability and child sleep problems at 9 months as well as parent anxiety and child difficult temperament. As the sample comprised genetically unrelated adopted infants the sleep disturbances cannot be explained by shared genes between parent and child.

Academic performance

Conflict between parents is also associated with children's poorer cognitive or intellectual abilities and poor school achievement (Harold et al., 2007). A range of processes explain these outcomes. One explanation focuses on sleep problems (El-Sheikh et al., 2007a), whereby sleep problems predict difficulties with attention and concentration at school. For example, a recent study found that sleep difficulties explained the impact of inter-parental conflict on children's academic performance, with children from high conflict homes achieving lower scores on maths, language, and verbal and nonverbal school ability scales (El-Sheikh et al., 2007a).

Another explanation centres on children's adjustment at school (Davies et al., 2008; Sturge-Apple et al., 2008; Bascoe et al., 2009). Children who develop negative representations of the relationship between their parents and with their parents are more likely to develop negative pictures of other relationships, including relationships with peers. In addition, the energy, attention and skills required to process hostile peer behaviour and the 'high alert' state they are in as a result of their internal pictures of relationships means children have limited resources left to manage their responses and stay focused on their school work (Bascoe et al., 2009). Longitudinal data following children from the start of school (age 6) in the USA highlights the significant role of children's representations of the inter-parental relationship in explaining attention difficulties (Davies et al., 2008), emotional and classroom difficulties two years later (Sturge-Apple et al., 2008) and overall school adjustment. Children's representations of the relationship between parents affected how they saw and processed events with peers at school (Bascoe et al., 2009).

Children's attributions about the causes and their role in conflict are also important. Children who blame themselves for inter-parental conflict are more likely to have poor academic attainment, after controlling for initial behaviour problems, than children who do not blame themselves (Harold et al., 2007). The impact of inter-parental conflict on those areas of children's wellbeing already discussed, such as behavioural problems and problems getting on with others, also serve to disrupt children's school life.

Chapter 5 sets out how the outcomes of exposure to conflict between parents for children may vary according to the child's age.

To summarise

- Although conflict between parents can affect children in a number of ways, a frequent outcome is the development of emotional or behavioural difficulties.
- Relationships can also be affected, with children prone to developing poor interpersonal skills. As a result, children and young people in high conflict homes may have difficulties getting on with others, such as parents, teachers, peers and romantic partners.
- Children are also at risk of a range of health difficulties, such as digestive problems, abdominal pains, headaches, fatigue and reduced growth. They may also suffer with sleep problems.
- Difficulties can extend into school, with children less able to settle, more likely to experience problems with peers, and less likely to achieve academically.

CHAPTER 4

HOW DOES INTER-PARENTAL CONFLICT AFFECT CHILDREN?

The previous chapter sets out how the distress children experience when exposed to conflict between parents can translate into long-term difficulties, including emotional and behavioural problems, troubled relationships and failure to settle and achieve at school (e.g. see Rhoades, 2008; Cummings and Davies, 2010). As the body of research documenting an association between a high conflict home and poor outcomes for children has grown, over the last decade research attention has turned to examining the mechanisms that explain these poor outcomes, the focus of this current chapter. Explanations fall broadly into two categories. First, inter-parental conflict affects parenting and the quality of the relationship between parent and child (i.e. conflict between parents 'spills over' to the parent–child relationship). Secondly, children's negative cognitive and emotional responses to conflict, including how they represent or perceive family relationships, make them vulnerable to adjustment difficulties.

Inter-parental conflict and troubled family relationships

One of the ways that inter-parental conflict influences children's adjustment is through its impact on parenting and the parent–child relationship (Schoppe-Sullivan et al., 2007; Cox et al., 2001; Erel and Burman, 1995). Distress in the couple relationship can be expressed through a range of unhelpful parenting behaviours, from highly intrusive and harsh parenting through to lax, inconsistent and emotionally unavailable parenting.

Harsh discipline and intrusive parenting

In keeping with a 'spillover' hypothesis, suggesting that negative emotions in the couple relationship spill over to the parent–child relationship(s), parenting in high conflict homes can be characterised by aggression, criticism, verbal and physical threat, yelling, hitting and shoving (Holden and Ritchie, 1991; Jenkins and Smith, 1991). A body of evidence links harsh parenting to children's externalising (Gonzales et al., 2000; Buehler and Gerard, 2002; Buehler et al., 2006; Benson et al., 2008; Harold et al., 2012) and internalising problems (Doyle and Markiewicz, 2005; Buehler et al., 2006) arising out of conflict between parents. Parents may also become psychologically controlling – attempting to influence children's thoughts, feelings and attitudes in line with their own expectations – again with deleterious outcomes for children (Krishnakumar et al., 2003; Doyle and Markiewicz, 2005; Buehler et al., 2006; Schoppe-Sullivan et al., 2007). For example, Buehler and colleagues found that psychologically intrusive parenting partly explained the link between inter-parental conflict and adolescents' emotional difficulties (Buehler et al., 2006; Benson et al., 2008).

Lax, inconsistent parenting

At the other end of the spectrum, parents in conflict may be inconsistent or indifferent, providing unstructured care and are either unaware of, or uninterested in, their children's activities and social world (Krishnakumar and Buehler, 2000). Pressure arising from inter-parental conflict can also put a strain on the co-parenting relationship, i.e. how partners support one another as parents in the care of their children (Cummings and Davies, 2010). Rather than work together in looking after their children, distressed parents tend to be hostile and competitive around family issues, upholding differing expectations and setting different standards. Inconsistent parenting increases the chances of greater parent–child conflict and has been linked to childhood adjustment difficulties (Gonzales et al., 2000; Benson et al., 2008). For example, Benson and colleagues (2008) found that inconsistent discipline partly explained the link between inter-parental conflict and adolescent internalising and externalising problems.

Emotionally unavailable, unsupportive parenting

In a similar vein, parents may struggle to remain emotionally available to their children when preoccupied with, and distressed by, conflict with a partner (Olson and Gorall, 2003; Rohner, 2004 cited in Benson et al., 2008). As a consequence, children may feel rejected, uncared for and lacking in parental approval, with long-term implications for wellbeing. For example, low levels of acceptance have been found to partly explain the link between inter-parental conflict and adolescents' internalising problems (Buehler et al., 2006; Benson et al., 2008).

Compensation, scapegoating, triangulation

In contrast to these generally negative patterns of behaviour, another perspective suggests that a parent who does not fulfil his or her emotional needs in the marital relationship may compensate for this by putting everything into their role as a parent. Therefore, the poorer the relationship between partners, the better the quality of the parent–child relationship (Erel and Burman, 1995). While it may seem that children will benefit from parents' attentiveness, this is unlikely to be the case (Cox et al., 2001). For example, a mother who throws herself into a relationship with her daughter to compensate for an unsatisfying marriage may abruptly withdraw this affection when the relationship with her partner improves – leaving her child on an emotional roller coaster of rejection and reconciliation (both mothers and fathers may behave in this way with children of either sex). Compensatory responses may also create unhealthy alliances within the family. For example, a parent may seek solace from one child, but be inattentive or harsh in their treatment of another.

Alternatively, parents may deny problems in their own relationship and focus instead on what parents perceive as the child's real or imagined problems – a process of scapegoating (Fauber et al., 1990) or detouring (Minuchin et al., 1978). Of course, children are upset at becoming the unjustified targets of their parents' anger and hostility but feel unable to change the situation.

Implications for children's emotional security and attachment

These patterns of parenting may result in the development of an insecure attachment for the child (sense of security between a child and caregiver) because parents caught up in conflict tend to be less able to respond to their infant's need for support, warmth and sensitivity (Davies et al., 2002). Older children whose parents appear hostile towards each other often report feeling less confident about their parents' relationship, their own relationship with their parents, and the long-term stability of the family (Shelton and Harold, 2008). Proponents of the Emotional Security theory (see below) suggest that this is the main way in which disrupted parenting resulting from conflict between parents affects children's psychological wellbeing. That is to say that inter-parental conflict creates parenting difficulties, which in turn undermine children's sense of security in the couple relationship and the parent–child bond (Cummings and Davies, 2010)

Processes that explain the negative impact of couple conflict on parenting

A number of theories have been proposed to explain how parenting and the parent–child relationship is affected.

Family systems theory

Family systems theory recognises the interdependence and mutual influence between individuals in a family. As well as the permeable 'boundary' that separates the family from the social world, boundaries also demarcate sub-systems, such as the relationship between the parents, or a parent–child relationship. Inter-parental conflict can spill over, challenge and even dissolve these boundaries, with a resultant impact on parenting and the parent–child relationship (Cox et al., 2001; Kerig and Swanson, 2009). Drawing on family systems theory, the spill-over hypothesis suggests that negative feelings and mood in the couple relationship are transferred into the parent–child relationship (Erel and Burman, 1995; Margolin et al., 2001). This may happen in different ways, from anger between parents being turned on children through to parents so exhausted and distracted by frequent quarrels that they are less emotionally available to their children (Volling and Belsky, 1991; Katz and Gottman, 1996). For example, one study found that mothers and fathers were 50% more likely to have a tense interaction with their children the day after a fight with a partner (Almeida et al., 1999). Furthermore, the transfer of emotion is not confined to a particular conflict event, rather, studies demonstrate that the emotional tone in one relationship, e.g. between parents, can influence other relationships within the family (Margolin et al., 2004).

Social modelling

Parents are important role models in children's lives whom they copy and from whom they learn. Social learning theory suggests that, because parents represent these important models, children copy the negative ways in which their parents relate to one another. Underlying the perspective is a suggestion that parents lack the basic interpersonal skills required for managing the couple relationship and parent–child relationship. If children observe their parents relating to one another in angry, hostile ways they may behave in the same way both within and outside of the family. They are also likely to feel less inhibited about behaving aggressively (Cox et al., 2001; Margolin et al., 2001). For example, one study found that parents of girls with conduct disorders were more hostile and aggressive than parents of girls without conduct disorders (Johnson and O'Leary, 1987).

Emotional, cognitive and behavioural responses to conflict: the child's perspective

If children are affected by marital discord only as a result of changes in parenting or parent–child relations, it might be expected that children would be affected irrespective of whether or not they actually observe their parents arguing. However, this does not appear to be the case. Rather, children who observe their parents argue are often more troubled than children who do not (Harold and Murch, 2005). Furthermore, studies also demonstrate that many children experience physiological changes in the face of inter-parental conflict, such as increases in cortisol levels and the activation of their bodies' fight or flight mechanisms (Cummings et al., 2007; Davies et al., 2008; Davies et al., 2009). Researchers have therefore developed and tested a set of explanations that capture the child's perspective to explain how inter-parental conflict may affect children's adjustment. These explanations focus on children's emotional and cognitive responses, that is to say, how children experience and make sense of inter-parental conflict and how they behave in response to that processing.

The role of cognitions and appraisals: cognitive-contextual framework

The cognitive-contextual framework (see Figure 4.1) (Grych and Fincham, 1990; Grych and Cardoza-Fernandes,

2001) suggests that children strive to understand (cognitive processing) and to cope with parental conflict because they find it stressful. If, as they try to cope, they develop an inappropriate understanding of the causes of their parents' relationship difficulties, for example, blame themselves for the conflict and develop harmful ways of coping with it, they can develop adjustment problems.

Grych and Fincham propose that children evaluate conflict in three ways, according to: i) its perceived threat i.e. how much will the conflict escalate and result in harm to the child or other family members, or even threaten the stability of the family; ii) the extent to which they blame themselves for their parents' rows; and iii) how well they feel able to cope (Grych and Cardoza-Fernandes, 2001).

The framework outlines two mental processing stages. Stage one, the primary processing stage, refers to the point at which children become aware that parents are rowing and experience an emotional response. The 'primary' stage may then lead to a more complex secondary processing stage, particularly if children perceive the conflict to be a threat. At this point the child attempts to understand why parents are rowing, what it might mean for their wellbeing and how they should cope with the conflict. How the child processes what is going on over these two stages is affected by their observation of the row; how intense it is, whether it is likely to be resolved, as well as how frequently parents are in conflict. These processing stages are not necessarily conscious, rather, processing is 'automatized' and takes place outside of awareness (Grych and Cardoza-Fernandes, 2001). Other contextual factors will also shape children's responses at this stage, including the nature/quality of the parent-child relationship(s), child gender, temperament, and history of exposure to conflict. Children who feel threatened by their parents' rows or who feel unable to cope experience more anxiety and helplessness. Children who believe they are the cause of their parents' arguments may develop low self-esteem and feel unable to cope with conflict at home and outside of the family (Grych and Fincham, 1990).

A number of studies have found evidence in support of the processes suggested in the cognitive-contextual framework (Grych et al., 2000; Grych et al., 2003; Fosco and Grych, 2007). For example, Grych et al. (2003) demonstrated that when children responded to conflicts by blaming themselves or by feeling threatened they were more vulnerable to internalising difficulties, such as depression and anxiety, and externalising problems, such as aggression and hostility. Different pathways were also apparent for girls and boys. Girls' feelings of threat increased the likelihood of depression and anxiety more so than for boys, while boys' feelings of self-blame and responsibility exacerbated their behavioural difficulties more so than for girls.

Emotional security theory

The emotional security theory (EST), drawing on attachment theory, provides a complementary perspective that highlights the importance of children's emotional reactions to conflict as well as their cognitive responses (see Figure 4.2). EST suggests that children's sense of emotional security in the family is threatened by inter-parental conflict which, in turn, increases their vulnerability to adjustment difficulties. For example, a row may seem threatening because it may signify, for the child, the end of the relationship between the parents or the end of the family unit. According to EST, children's sense of emotional security is threatened in two ways. First, conflict threatens how children perceive the relationship between parents i.e.

Figure 4.1: Cognitive – contextual framework

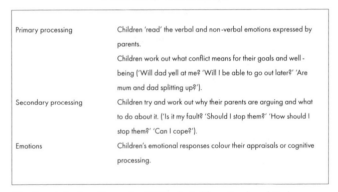

(Grych and Cardoza-Fernandes, 2001 adapted from Grych and Fincham, 1990)

the couple relationship. Secondly, inter-parental conflict affects how they see their own relationship with their parents and whether that relationship can continue to offer security. Although overlapping, Cummings and Davies argue that the child's security in the couple relationship is distinct from the parent–child relationship (Cummings and Davies, 1996; Cummings and Davies, 2010).

Cummings and Davies (1994) suggest that conflict between parents disrupts three areas of children's emotional functioning:

1. First, inter-parental conflict triggers an **emotional reaction** such as anger, sadness, fear, relief etc. The nature and depth of emotional arousal, coupled with how well children can manage these emotions, is one factor that affects the impact of conflict on children's adjustment.
2. A second factor is how children **perceive** or 'represent' family relationships as a result of the conflict. That is, conflict between parents may leave children feeling anxious about the potential for conflict between the parent and the child, or other siblings. This results in a perception that family relationships are insecure.
3. A third element focuses on how children **manage** their exposure to parental conflict – so how they behave in response. For example, a child may try to intervene to stop the row, alternatively he or she may decide to keep out of the way.

How conflict affects children's long-term emotional and behavioural wellbeing is influenced by the extent to which children's feelings of security are undermined and how well they can manage the emotional disruption. Unhelpful emotional responses can result in long-term emotional and behavioural problems (Cummings et al., 2006; Cummings and Davies, 2010).

A number of studies provide support for the emotional security theory (Davies and Cummings, 1994) across different ages of children (Harold et al., 2004; Cummings et al., 2006; El-Sheikh et al., 2008). For example, Cummings and colleagues (2006) found conflict between parents characterised by verbal aggression and overt hostility was

Figure 4.2: The emotional security theory

(Cummings and Davies, 2010)

associated with greater child emotional insecurity in two independent samples of children. A year later, greater emotional insecurity was linked to internalising problems among adolescents and both internalising and externalising problems for young school-aged children.

Complementary theories

The emotional security theory and the cognitive-contextual framework are the two main theories, focusing on a child's perspective, put forward and tested to explain the mechanisms behind the impact of inter-parental conflict on children's development. Other theories have also been developed which reflect some of these elements but differ in scope or emphasis. For example, the

Emotion specific theory also highlights the importance of children's emotional, cognitive and behavioural responses (Crockenberg and Langrock, 2001). However, the theory places less emphasis on the role of emotional security and more emphasis on how children evaluate and respond to the potential impact of conflict on their specific goals.

The *family–wide perspective* (Harold and Conger, 1997; Harold et al., 2004) also recognises the importance of children's cognitive and emotional responses but stresses the importance of how children's perceptions of parents' behaviour towards one another affects children's perceptions and expectations about how their parents will behave toward them. That is to say, children who have witnessed inter-parental conflict interpret parent–child conflict as more threatening than children who have not experienced similar levels of conflict between parents. In turn, children's perceptions of and experience of parent–child conflict affects their psychological wellbeing.

A combined perspective

Rather than being seen as competing theories, research over the last decade has served to find ways to integrate the main cognitive and emotional security perspectives. For example, in a longitudinal study, Harold and colleagues (2004) showed that children's cognitions and emotions work together. More recently, Fosco and Grych (2008) found that children's emotional reactions to conflict (rather than the broader notion of emotional security), their cognitive responses and perception of being caught in the middle or being involved in the conflict, all helped to explain children's externalising and internalising problems. In this, as in other studies, researchers were able to map distinct pathways linking particular responses to particular outcomes. Children who saw conflict as a threat were more likely to develop internalising problems. Self-blame and emotional distress were linked to both internalising and externalising difficulties.

The complementary nature of the different theories is borne out in the findings of a recent meta-analysis which evaluated the strength of evidence for the role of cognitions, negative emotions, behavioural responses and physiological reactions in explaining the link between inter-parental conflict and children's adjustment (Rhoades, 2008). Rhoades (2008) found support for all four perspectives, although cognitive and emotional responses were the most powerful explanations in linking conflict between parents with negative outcomes for children. Taken together, the theories highlight the 'mental architecture' underpinning children's reactions to conflict (Harold and Murch, 2005) and the importance of understanding children's perspectives in explaining the impact of inter-parental conflict on children's development.

Integrating perspectives has also extended to our understanding of how disrupted parenting, arising from inter-parental conflict, and children's emotional and cognitive responses, work together to explain how a high conflict home can spell trouble for children (Davies et al., 2002; Fosco and Grych, 2008; Sturge-Apple et al., 2008). For example, Davies and colleagues (2002) found that children's levels of security in the relationship between parents (emotional security theory) and in the parent–child relationship together explained the impact of conflict between parents on children's development. In particular, children exposed to poor parenting as a result of conflict between parents, such as lack of warmth, poor behavioural control and high psychological control, were more likely to develop insecure attachments to their parents and these insecure attachments put them at risk of adjustment difficulties.

A critical question in understanding how everyday family experiences help or hurt children's emotional and/or behavioural development is to go beyond simply describing the components or features of parenting and/or inter-parental conflict that appear consonant with positive or negative outcomes for children, to describing how these factors affect children's development.

Inter-parental conflict and children's early brain development

An emerging area of research examining the effects of inter-parental conflict on children highlights how acrimonious relations between parents may affect children's early brain development, specifically neurobiological processes critical to healthy emotional and cognitive development.

Specifically relating to the development of antisocial behaviour problems in children, a recent theoretical model suggests that early environmental adversity (e.g. inter-parental conflict and violence), increases children's propensity to develop antisocial behaviour problems through its impact on specific neurobiological processes, which in turn affect children's emotional and cognitive development, which then lead to elevated rates of antisocial behaviour problems (Van Goozen et al., 2007). While research in this area is at a fairly embryonic stage, initial findings suggest that a region of brain activity marked by the hypothalamic pituitary adrenal axis (HPA) located in the area of the brain known as the prefrontal cortex, may be particularly susceptible to early environmental stress. Broadly defined, the HPA axis is a stress-sensitive neurobiological system that works with other systems to mobilise the body to respond to real or perceived threat. The early social environment has been shown to affect the HPA axis and to lead to subsequent emotional and behavioural difficulties in children. Inter-parental conflict is increasingly recognised as a significant early social environmental influence that may affect children's psychological development (Van Goozen et al., 2008).

Sensitisation: don't children get used to fighting parents?

Although it is tempting to speculate that children get used to their parents' quarrels, both the cognitive contextual perspective and the emotional security perspective provide strong grounds, and good evidence, that rather than get used to conflict, the more conflict occurs, the more sensitive children become to it and, as a result, they are more vulnerable to its effects (Cummings and Davies, 2002; Cummings and Merrilees, 2009). This is because although children's short-term reactions to conflict e.g. distracting a parent or withdrawing, may serve to help them manage their feelings and sense of threat to themselves or the security of the family, over the long term they develop unhelpful patterns of behaviour that can be detrimental to themselves and that may be carried over to other settings and relationships, for example with peers or teachers.

To summarise

- Inter-parental conflict affects children in two key ways. First, children are affected because conflict affects how couples parent and the quality of the relationship between parent and child. Parenting may be affected in a number of respects, with parents adopting a range of behaviours from highly intrusive and hostile parenting through to lax, uninterested parenting, all of which are associated with negative developmental outcomes for children.
- Secondly, how children understand, experience and respond to conflict between parents is also important, each with implications for the parent–child relationship and, in turn, children's development.
- Different theories have been put forward to specify the exact nature in which children's reactions to conflict affects their wellbeing – including the cognitive-contextual framework, emotional security theory, emotion specific theory and family-wide perspective. Although theories place different emphasis on different aspects of the processes at work, the theories are complementary. Taken together they demonstrate that children's cognitive, emotional, behavioural and physiological responses to conflict explain how inter-parental conflict affects children's adjustment.
- Emerging research also points to the influence of inter-parental conflict on early brain development, a critical phase in the development of normal emotional and cognitive functioning.
- It is also the case that rather than get used to conflict, the more children are exposed to conflict the more sensitive they become to its presence.

CHAPTER 5

RISK AND RESILIENCE: WHY ARE SOME CHILDREN AFFECTED MORE THAN OTHERS?

Conflict between parents can have a long-lasting impact on children's wellbeing and development. However, as noted in Chapter 1, some children may be exposed to similar levels of hostility and aggression between parents and remain relatively unscathed by it. A comprehensive understanding of the impact of parental conflict therefore requires consideration as to why some children are more vulnerable to its impact than others. Moreover, identifying the mechanisms that explain why some children experience serious difficulties in the context of inter-parental conflict, while other children seem relatively unaffected (i.e. resilient) enables us to develop more effective support targeted at children and families most vulnerable and at risk.

This is vividly demonstrated by research into the processes occurring within the family when families experience economic pressure; a recognised risk factor for children (Conger et al., 1999). According to one well-supported theoretical model, under the strain of economic pressure parents are vulnerable to developing depression. Parental depression increases the likelihood of increased conflict and violence between parents, which in turn undermines parenting, thereby increasing the risk of children developing mental health difficulties (Conger et al., 1994). The theoretical model highlights the role of inter-parental conflict as a mediator, or vehicle through to harsh parenting practices, which in turn influence children's psychological outcomes as a result of the emotional strain of coping with difficult financial circumstances. This model focuses on economic pressure, but similar processes can apply in the case of other risk factors (e.g. parental divorce). These carefully researched explanatory models are helpful in isolating and understanding, not only the factors that may trigger increased inter-parental conflict, but also in understanding how inter-parental conflict as a factor in and of itself helps to explain poor developmental outcomes for children.

This chapter explores those factors which leave some children at risk and others resilient to the impact of conflict between parents. These factors are divided into i) the characteristics of the child, ii) characteristics of the family (including generational cycles of conflict), and iii) social, cultural or other factors outside of the family.

Child characteristics

Sex of parent and sex of child

The sex of the child and the sex of the parent and how these interact are all factors that may help to explain why some children fare better than others. Some early research appeared to suggest that boys may be more vulnerable to the impact of inter-parental conflict than girls. This is likely to have been a result of a greater propensity for boys to develop externalising rather than internalising difficulties and the greater ease of measuring and observing externalising outcomes. More recent studies show boys and girls may react to and experience inter-parental conflict differently but with equally deleterious outcomes for both boys and girls (Grych et al., 2003).

For example, girls appear more likely than boys to respond to inter-parental conflict by blaming themselves (Kerig et al., 1998), taking too much responsibility for repairing family relationships (Gore et al., 1993), feeling caught in the middle (Buchanan et al., 1991), and feeling compelled to intervene in the row (El-Sheikh et al., 1996; El-Sheikh and Reiter, 1996). Whilst both boys and girls may see conflict as a threat, girls are more likely to see it as a threat to family relationships and harmony, whereas boys are likely to see it as a threat to themselves (Grych et al., 2003).

Differences are also apparent at different developmental stages. For example, girls may be more susceptible to family stress during adolescence while boys may be more vulnerable, particularly to externalising difficulties, when they are younger (Davies and Lindsay, 2001). A number of mechanisms are thought to explain different responses and vulnerability to inter-parental conflict among girls and boys.

Different characteristics of boys and girls

A set of mechanisms surrounds the different characteristics of boys and girls. For example, boys are believed to have weaker neuropsychological and psychobiological systems, leaving them more susceptible to the stressful impact of inter-parental conflict (Emery, 1982). Differences may also be found in some of the developmental transitions boys and girls must navigate as well as the timing of those transitions. For example, girls are more likely to find the challenge of puberty combined with the move to a larger, more impersonal secondary school more stressful than boys (Windle, 1992). To some extent, girls and boys are socialised differently which may also partly account for differences in vulnerability to inter-parental conflict. For example, girls are thought to be more geared towards social networks and relationships than boys, with girls more likely to show concern for the welfare of others and interpersonal connectedness. This increases the risk that girls will feel caught in the middle of parental problems and responsible for their resolution. Boys, it is argued, are encouraged to be more self-interested, autonomous and self-directed. Different sex roles may result in girls and boys dealing with their distress in different ways, with girls more prone to depression and anxiety as they attempt to keep the peace at home. Boys, on the other hand, may respond to the perceived threat of conflict in the home by sending their concerns 'outwards', through aggression or other behavioural problems, in order to re-establish their authority (Davies and Lindsay, 2001).

Different responses to expression and resolution of conflict

There is some indication that girls and boys respond differently to certain aspects of conflict. In keeping with their concern for maintaining harmonious relationships, girls appear to be more sensitive to whether and how conflict has been resolved (El-Sheikh and Cummings, 1995; El-Sheikh et al., 1996 cited Davies and Lindsay, 2001). Boys, on the other hand, due to a concern for self-protection, may be more sensitive to highly aggressive and violent conflict because of the potential threat to their own wellbeing (Davies and Lindsay, 2001).

Conflict affects mothers' and fathers' parenting differently

Conflict between partners can also affect each partner and how they parent differently. In general, fathers respond to distress in the couple relationship with negativity, by withdrawing and disengaging (Katz and Gottman, 1996; Lindahl et al., 1997 cited in Davies and Lindsay, 2001). Overall, the father-child relationship appears more vulnerable to the impact of a troubled couple relationship than the mother-child relationship (Cummings and O'Reilly, 1997). Mothers are more able to compartmentalise their roles although there may also be a tendency for mothers to become more intrusive with their children and to compensate for difficulties in the couple relationship by over-investing in the relationship with their children (Cox et al., 2001).

In distressed relationships, mothers and fathers appear to treat an opposite sex child differently from a child who is of the same sex as the parent (Cummings and O'Reilly, 1997). Mothers may become more hostile towards their sons while fathers can become more withdrawn and avoidant towards their daughters (Kerig et al., 1993; Kitzmann, 2000). Daughters' greater assertiveness, control and defiance in interactions with fathers who are in distressed relationships (Kerig et al., 1993) may be an attempt to gain the involvement and attention of the father. One reason that parents may treat the opposite sex child in the same way they treat the partner is because they perceive similarities between the child and partner (Osborne and Fincham, 1996).

Girls and boys feel challenged by hostility towards a parent of the same sex

The picture is further complicated by the tendency for girls and boys to identify with the same sex parent. Because of this affiliation toward the same sex parent, children may react more strongly to the opposite parent's conflict behaviours and therefore perceive hostility towards the parent of the same gender as an attack on themselves (Davies and Lindsay, 2001).

Age/developmental stage

The roles of age and developmental stage as moderators are also complex. A recent meta-analysis of studies found that the association between conflict and child outcomes was stronger for older children compared with younger children on all measures of psychological adjustment included in the study, and for six outcome measures there was no significant impact at all for young children (Rhoades, 2008). This finding makes sense given the emphasis on the importance of children's appraisals of conflict and coping strategies in the main theories. For example, younger children may lack the cognitive abilities to generate and process unhelpful thoughts about or appraisals of inter-parental conflict (Grych et al., 2003). Alternatively, young children may appraise what is going on while conflict is occurring but stop thinking about it once the conflict is resolved. Rumination over what has happened may increase the risk of developing more generalised, persistent behaviour problems (Rhoades, 2008). One study found that young adolescents were more able than 7-9 year olds to 'read' couples' emotional cues to determine whether a conflict had been resolved (Davies et al., 1996). On the other hand, much of the research on cognitions has been conducted with children over seven, and it may also be the case that we need to find more appropriate ways of capturing younger children's cognitive reactions (Ablow and Measelle, 2009).

Another consideration is the interplay of different factors at key developmental stages. At any given developmental stage, some factors may increase children's vulnerability while other factors may mitigate that risk. For example, pre-schoolers are more disposed to fear, self-blame and threat in response to conflict (e.g. Jouriles et al., 2000) and they are limited in the range of coping strategies they can adopt to regulate their feelings (e.g. El-Sheikh and Cummings, 1995). Compared to older children and adolescents, however, preschoolers are less sensitive to adult problems because they have not been exposed to them for as long as older children. Preschoolers are also less likely to try and mediate conflicts whereas older children may get involved. Getting involved in inter-parental conflict increases the risk of externalising and internalising difficulties (Grych et al., 2004; Gerard et al., 2005; Franck and Buehler, 2007) and increases the chances of conflict between parents and children (Buehler and Gerard, 2002).

It is also possible that older children in high conflict homes may have witnessed more conflict over their lifetime than younger children and, as noted earlier, become more sensitive to its impact. Poorer outcomes for older children may therefore reflect greater exposure to conflict rather than developmental stage or age differences (Davies et al., 1999). However, sensitisation cannot completely account for differences according to age. A recent meta-analysis of studies examining children's adjustment to conflict found differences between older and younger children (under 10) even after taking account of their level of exposure to inter-parental conflict (Rhoades, 2008).

Temperament

Another important influence is child temperament. Children with a difficult temperament (e.g. more intense, less adaptable, prone to negative mood) may be more vulnerable to inter-parental conflict (Davies and Cummings, 1994; Davies and Windle, 2001; Ramos et al., 2005; Whiteside-Mansell et al., 2009). For example, in a longitudinal study of infants from 4 months through to 30 months, infants prone to moodiness and irritability (high in negative emotionality) from high conflict homes developed more serious behaviour problems compared to children with more positive temperaments (low in negative emotionality) (Pauli-Pott and Beckmann, 2007). However, it is also the case that exposure to inter-parental conflict can lead to emotional difficulties or a negative outlook (Schermerhorn et al., 2007).

On the other hand, some temperamental traits appear to protect children from the impact of inter-parental conflict. One study comparing adolescents in high conflict homes found that adolescents with a more hopeful outlook were less likely to develop internalising symptoms compared to adolescents who had a less hopeful outlook (Buehler and Welsh, 2009). Effortful control – the ability to regulate attention, behaviour and emotions – may also be important (Whitson and El-Sheikh, 2003). Children high in effortful control appear less vulnerable to the harmful impact of inter-parental conflict because they can observe conflict from a more detached perspective (David and Murphy, 2007).

One reason that temperament may be important is that children with difficult temperaments are more sensitive and reactive to repeated exposure to conflict and hence find it harder to maintain a sense of security in the face of parental conflict (Davies and Windle, 2001). It may also be the case that children with a difficult temperament may rely on unhelpful ways of coping with conflict and therefore struggle to regulate their emotional reactions (Grych and Fincham, 1990). For example, in one study, young people who had trouble regulating their emotions were more distressed by exposure to simulated adult conflicts than adolescents who were more able to manage their emotions (David and Murphy, 2004).

'Difficult' children may also both pose a strain on the couple relationship and the relationship between parent and child, leading to negative cycles of relating. Children with difficult temperaments may challenge already fragile family relationships with a resulting increase in conflict and exposure to conflict (Davies and Cummings, 1994; Davies and Windle, 2001). For example, Schermerhorn and colleagues (2007) found that where children responded to parental conflict by acting up, behaving aggressively and shouting, conflict between parents increased over time.

Coping strategies

Coping strategies play both a mediating and moderating role in linking inter-parental conflict to children's adjustment (e.g. Shelton and Harold, 2008). As well as being a vehicle through which conflict can affect children's wellbeing (see Chapter 4) coping strategies can also buffer or protect children from its deleterious impact (Kerig, 2001). Although researchers have adopted a number of different ways of conceptualising coping strategies, one of the more common categorisations is to distinguish between 'emotion-focused' coping and 'problem-focused' coping. Problem-focused strategies encapsulate attempts to shape or control what is going on and broadly describes attempts to intervene in the conflict, for example, by mediating between parents, creating a distraction or taking sides. In contrast, emotion-focused strategies reflect children's attempts to change their emotional state and alleviate the distress by avoidance, escaping, reframing their understanding of it, support seeking or distancing themselves (Cummings and Davies, 2002).

In general, emotion-focused strategies are associated with better adjustment than problem-solving strategies, which may involve the child in the argument (Kerig, 2001). However, findings are not completely straightforward. The moderating role of different coping strategies appears to vary for boys and girls and according to the particular outcome under scrutiny (Nicolotti et al., 2003; Kerig, 2001). Some strategies, such as support seeking, do not appear to be consistently helpful, with some finding evidence for its effectiveness (Nicolotti et al., 2003) while others have found no evidence (Shelton and Harold, 2007).

Physiological reactivity

One area where research has developed over the last 10 years is in our understanding of the role that physiological responses play in linking inter-parental conflict and children's psychological adjustment (El Sheikh and Erath, 2011). Their role is complex. On the one hand, some systems are established early in life and remain stable over time, such as vagal tone (i.e. baseline heart rate), and serve to moderate children's responses to inter-parental conflict (Steinberg and Avenevoli, 2000). Other systems change over time, for example responses to on-going exposure to a stressful home environment can set up unhelpful physiological reactions to stress. The wear and tear on the physiological systems arising out of less adaptive responses to stress take a toll on children's psychological functioning (Davies et al., 2009).

The autonomic nervous system (ANS) with its two branches, the sympathetic and parasympathetic nervous systems, is one important pathway linking inter-parental conflict and children's wellbeing. Although the two branches work together, a rule of thumb is that the sympathetic nervous system (SNS) regulates our bodies' reactions to stress or threat and accelerates heart rate and increases physiological arousal. The parasympathetic nervous system (PNS) is involved in soothing and calming. It maintains the body at rest and decelerates heart rate and reduces physiological reactivity. When these two systems work together, children are less vulnerable to developing externalising difficulties in the context of a high conflict home compared with when the two systems act in opposition to one another (El-Sheikh et al., 2009). Research has also focused on the functioning of particular aspects of the ANS.

Vagal tone and vagal regulation

Research has consistently identified vagal tone (baseline heart rate) and vagal regulation (how the body regulates the heart in stressful situations) as important moderators in children's reactions to inter-parental conflict (Porges, 2007; El-Sheikh and Erath, 2011). Children with high vagal tone or increased vagal withdrawal (where the heart rate is increased in order to cope with a demanding/stressful situation) are less at risk of psychological maladjustment than children with low vagal tone or vagal augmentation when faced with conflict between parents (El-Sheikh et al., 2001; Leary and Katz, 2006; El-Sheikh and Whitson, 2006; El Sheikh and Erath, 2011). This 'protective' effect is attributed to the way in which the parasympathetic nervous system helps children to regulate their emotions and social engagement in stressful situations (Porges, 2007, cited in El-Sheikh and Erath, 2011).

Skin conductance reactivity

Skin conductance level reactivity (SCL-R) measures changes in sweat/heat levels in the hands. Sweat glands respond to the stimulation of the sympathetic nervous system and assessing SCL-R provides another measure of the body's sense of stress or threat in the face of inter-parental conflict. Higher SCL-R predicts poorer adjustment for children in high conflict homes. However risks appear to depend on both age and sex, with higher SCL-R a stronger vulnerability factor for girls compared with boys (El-Seikh, 2005; El-Sheikh et al., 2007). Findings for boys are more complicated and vary according to psychological outcome, parenting style and developmental stage (El Sheikh and Erath, 2011).

Other physiological systems

Other physiological systems are also important, including the body's hormonal response to stress, through the release, for example, of cortisol. Lower levels of cortisol reactivity are linked with externalising problems in the context of conflict between parents (Davies et al., 2007; El Sheikh et al., 2008).

Family characteristics

Factors within the family, such as sibling relationships or the family's emotional tone, may also diminish or increase children's vulnerability to adverse outcomes in high conflict homes. Additionally, cycles of conflict and the generational transmission of behavioural and genetic characteristics may play a role.

Sibling relationships

Siblings play an important role in each other's wellbeing, shaping many aspects of one another's development, including social competence, peer relations and emotional health (Dunn and Davies, 2001; Dunn, 2002). Siblings in the same family may be exposed to different levels of conflict and experience conflict differently (Richmond and Stocker, 2003), with older children and boys possibly being exposed to more physical and overt conflict than younger siblings and girls (Grych et al., 2003). One study found that levels of exposure explained differences in outcomes for siblings (Richmond and Stocker, 2003). However, another reported that it was not differences in exposure to conflict that explained different outcomes for siblings, rather it was the particular characteristics and vulnerabilities of each child (Jenkins et al., 2005).

Whether or not siblings are exposed to different levels of conflict, a warm sibling relationship can buffer children from the impact of conflict (Grass et al., 2007; Modry-Mandell et al., 2007). However, sibling relationships can also come under stress in the context of conflict, with researchers demonstrating a link between inter-parental conflict and conflict between siblings (see Dunn and Davies, 2001). For example, one study that observed family dynamics in distressed families over a two week period found that siblings were more likely to fight 24 hours after their parents had been rowing (Margolin et al., (1996) cited Jenkins et al., 2005). Different mechanisms may explain this. For example, siblings may deflect parental anger from themselves to another sibling, one sibling may become the scapegoat, or form an alliance with one parent (Cox et al., 2001).

Family functioning and parent–child relations

The broader family environment and emotional tone of the family can also play a protective or exacerbating role. One study found that children were more vulnerable to maladjustment arising from exposure to conflict between parents in families characterised by higher levels of negative emotion compared with families who were less marked by negativity (Fosco and Grych, 2007). In a similar vein, high levels of parent–child conflict (Gordis et al., 1997, 2001; Crockenberg and Langrock, 2001; El Sheikh and Elmore-Staton, 2004) and harsh parenting (Frosch and Mangelsdorf, 2001) are both factors which increase children's vulnerability to the impact of inter-parental conflict. On the other hand, a supportive relationship between parent and child (Davies and Windle, 2001; Davies et al., 2002; Grych et al., 2004; DeBoard-Lucas et al., 2010) and secure maternal or paternal attachment (El Sheikh and Elmore-Staton, 2004; DeBoard-Lucas et al., 2010) can help to buffer children. One reason that positive relationships and positive emotional expression can buffer children is because they are less likely to blame themselves for discord between parents and less likely to feel they should intervene (Fosco and Grych, 2007; DeBoard-Lucas et al., 2010).

One study assessed the impact of conflict in the context of four different family types in keeping with a family systems approach: 'cohesive families', characterised by warmth, affection and flexible, well-defined boundaries; 'disengaged families', demonstrating high levels of adversity and low levels of support; 'enmeshed families', characterised by high levels of discord and weakly maintained subsystem boundaries; and 'adequate families', defined by high parental psychological control, low levels of conflict and high levels of warmth (Davies et al., 2004). Family type was found to moderate the link between inter-parental conflict, emotional insecurity and internalising symptoms. Children in 'enmeshed families' exhibited the most widespread signs of insecurity in the inter-parental relationship despite being exposed to similar levels of inter-parental discord as children in 'disengaged families'. One reason may be that children interpret the meaning of conflict differently depending on the broader functioning of the family system. For example, children in 'enmeshed families' may feel more insecure in the inter-parental relationship because of the troubled parenting they have experienced.

There is also some evidence that fathers have a distinctive, protective role to play, with some studies finding that a close relationship with a father buffers children from the impact of inter-parental conflict (Crockenberg et al., 2007; Grych et al., 2004). Conversely, other studies suggest that the association between fathers' parenting and child outcomes in the context of inter-parental conflict may be more strained compared with the same association between mothers and children. Interestingly, this difference in association is apparent irrespective of whether mothers, fathers and children are genetically related or not. This highlights the differential role of the father–child and mother–child relationships on child outcomes when parents are embroiled in a hostile inter-parental relationship (Harold et al., 2012), and endorses an emerging evidence base signifying the important role that both mothers and fathers play in understanding family influences on child development.

Conflict style: staying with the positives

Chapter two also highlights the role that conflict style and resolution can play. Children may be more or less vulnerable depending on how parents argue and if and how arguments are resolved. Children are also less vulnerable if parents manage to interact with warmth, humour and affection when they argue. Research suggests that the balance between 'positive' and 'negative' ways of interacting during conflict can differentiate between couples who are likely to separate and those likely to stay together. A ratio of five positives to one negative is seen as healthy or protective (Driver et al., 2003). Diluting the impact of destructive conflict with warm, positive interactions is also important for children.

Family stress

Inter-parental conflict is one of a number of family stressors, such as socioeconomic status, parental mental health, and alcohol or substance misuse, associated with poor outcomes for children. Some studies suggest that the association between inter-parental conflict and child adjustment difficulties is stronger in families with additional problems, i.e. that other family stress exacerbates the impact of conflict. This is possibly because children must deal with the impact of multiple family stressors (e.g. Jouriles et al., 1991) which act as cumulative risk factors, so that the combined risk of a number of factors is greater than the risk for each individual family pressure (Appleyard et al., 2005). It is also the case that couples coping with a range of pressures are more likely to experience discord and conflict, which in turn affects their ability to parent and their children's wellbeing (Conger et al., 1992).

Parental depression

Understanding the relationship between children's adjustment, parental depression and inter-parental conflict is not straightforward. A number of factors are important, including genetic predispositions, environmental factors such as parenting and family climate, and whether inter-parental conflict precedes or follows one or both parents' depression (e.g. Davies and Cummings, 2006; Cummings and Davies, 2010). Despite the complexity there is a persuasive body of evidence suggesting that conflict between parents is the linking factor between parental depression and poor outcomes for children (Downey and Coyne, 1990; Cummings et al., 2005; Blodgett Salafia et al., 2008). Conflict is more common in depressed couples (Cummings and Davies, 1994; Du Rocher Schudlich et al., 2004), and one study found that a depressed conflict style was associated with children's internalising symptoms while destructive and constructive styles were not (Du Rocher Schudlich and Cummings, 2003). Although children of parents with depression are significantly more likely to develop psychological problems than other children (Cummings and Davies, 2010), this is not all down to genes. Exposure to marital conflict appears to be a trigger for the emergence of depression. Children from high conflict homes with a family history of depression are at greater risk of developing depression than children from less discordant homes with a family history of depression (Rice et al., 2006).

Parental alcohol and substance abuse

Parental drinking appears to be another factor that increases risks for poor adjustment through its impact on family relationships. One study found parental alcohol abuse was linked to children's externalising and internalising problems through negative marital conflict and poorer parenting (Schact et al., 2009). These findings are echoed in other studies (Keller et al., 2005; Keller et al., 2008). Parental substance abuse also appears to increase the risk of child maladjustment related to conflict. Children living with drug abusing fathers were found to have more emotional and behavioural problems than either children living with alcoholic fathers or those living with non-substance-abusing fathers. This was associated with a higher frequency of physical violence and greater incidence of inter-parental conflict witnessed by children in families characterised by substance abuse (Faks-Stewart et al., 2004). The complex problems relating to parental alcohol and substance abuse and the impact on children suggest that targeted interventions to tackle these issues should also include a component which covers inter-parental conflict (Kelley and Fals-Stewart, 2002; see Chapter 6)

Socioeconomic pressure and family stress

Impoverished socioeconomic circumstances are associated with a range of negative outcomes for children (e.g. Repetti et al., 2002, review), in part because socioeconomic pressures are associated with increases in conflict between parents and increased parenting difficulties. Conger and colleagues (1992) have provided a comprehensive model to explain how socioeconomic pressures create negative outcomes for children through a chain of stressors, with economic worries triggering parental depression and depression creating increased couple conflict and undermining effective parenting. Socioeconomic pressure therefore increases the risk of children experiencing negative outcomes as a result of exposure to inter-parental conflict.

Although socioeconomic pressures can increase the risk of children's exposure to inter-parental conflict, studies have found a consistent link between inter-parental conflict and child outcomes regardless of socioeconomic status (Buehler and Gerard, 2002; El-Sheikh et al., 2008). That is, children are vulnerable to the impact of a high conflict home regardless of their parents' socioeconomic situations.

Cycles of conflict: transmitting behaviour across generations

Part of this developing understanding has included improved recognition of the ways in which conflicted family processes are transmitted from one generation to the next (intergenerational transmission). It is increasingly recognised that the origins of family violence, and in particular patterns of inter-parental conflict management, are learned early in life (i.e. children are exposed to destructive inter-parental conflict) and then carried into later in life (perpetrating destructive inter-parental conflict behaviour as an adult) (Harold et al., 2012).

Hypotheses offered to explain the intergenerational transmission of these destructive behaviours fall into three primary groupings: (1) genetic transmission (Plomin, 1990); (2) exposure to negative family environments that promote the maintenance of adverse psychological symptoms and behaviours across generations (Capaldi et al., 2003); and (3) the interplay between the two, so that individuals with specific genetic characteristics who are exposed to adverse environments are at greatest risk of psychopathology and therefore more likely to perpetuate destructive behaviours across generations (Rutter, 2006).

Recent evidence specifically relating to the transmission of hostile inter-parental behaviours, suggests that even when other factors such as parent mental ill health (e.g. aggression, depression) and genetic factors linking parents and children are considered, hostile behaviours expressed by parents have significant implications for levels of aggression in children (even when children are not genetically related to their rearing/caregiving parents; Harold et al., 2013). Identifying these processes informs the development of interventions aimed at correcting patterns of hostile conflict management early in life that can improve the lives of children today as well as promote positive family relationships tomorrow.

Do genes explain effects on children?

A limitation of past research examining family influences on children's mental health outcomes is that the vast majority of research has been conducted with biologically related parents and children. Studies that involve only biologically related family members make it difficult to understand the relative roles of shared genetic and/ or environmental backgrounds within families in child mental health outcomes. That is, in examining the relative role of genetic and environmental factors on children's psychological symptoms, genes may not only affect aspects of a child's emotional wellbeing or behavior but may also affect the family conditions or environment that children experience, such as a child's exposure to inter-parental conflict or hostile parenting practices. For example, children of divorced parents are at increased risk for a variety of negative psychological outcomes, as outlined earlier in this chapter. Whereas this association could be explained by exposure to acrimonious conflict between parents before, during and after divorce, it could also be explained by a shared genetic predisposition for negative emotionality and relationship problems (D'Onofrio et al., 2007). This raises the question as to whether exposure to acrimonious inter-parental relations is sufficient as an influence in its own right to affect children's psychological development or whether it is the result of children's biological predisposition towards psychological difficulties arising from their genetic makeup.

Recent studies have attempted to address this question by using samples of parents and children that are not genetically related, thereby providing insight into the role of the family environment as a unique influence on children's psychological development, over and above explanations confounded by the problem of common genetic factors (Harold et al., 2010; Mannering et al., 2011; Rhoades et al., 2011). For example, Mannering et al. (2011) examined the direction of effects between parental relationship instability (e.g., general quarrelling and relationship dissatisfaction) and children's sleep problems (e.g., restlessness and irritability) when children were 9 months and 18 months respectively. The researchers found that parental relationship instability when children were 9 months old predicted children's sleep problems at 18 months. Sleep problems did not predict relationship difficulties, thereby allowing the conclusion that relationship problems affect children's early sleep patterns (critical for early brain development), not the other way around. This study utilised a sample of children adopted at birth into non-family member homes, which means that the link between parental relationship instability and children's sleep problems cannot be explained by common genetic factors. Similarly, Harold et al. (2010), utilising a sample of parents and children where children were born through in vitro fertilisation, looked at the role of parenting behaviours, such as warmth or hostility, in explaining the links between parent psychopathology and child psychopathology (e.g. aggression). Results suggest that harsh parenting practices explained associations between parent aggression and child aggression among genetically related and genetically unrelated mother–child and father–child pairings. The fact that these associations were statistically significant in the genetically unrelated parent–child groupings means that these associations (parent aggression, harsh parenting practices, child aggression) cannot be explained by common underlying genetic factors, thereby affirming the role of parenting as a salient environmental mechanism through which parental aggression affects child aggression.

Studies that use these research designs offer ground-breaking potential when it comes to identifying factors within the family that have a unique influence on children's psychological development. They also have major implications for the next generation of family focused intervention programmes aimed at promoting positive outcomes for children within a family context. Research to date on effective interventions to support parents in conflict is reported in Chapter 6. Developing effective interventions in support of family relationships is a crucial response to the evidence on the links between inter-parental conflict and children's wellbeing and emerging knowledge that this association cannot be explained by shared genetic makeup alone.

Extra-familial characteristics

Race and ethnicity

Much of the research on inter-parental conflict has involved families from European American backgrounds and there are concerns about how applicable findings are to other ethnic groups and cultures (Lindahl et al., 2004). However, although limited by number, studies that have used more varied samples have found a consistent link between inter-parental conflict and children's adjustment regardless of ethnicity (Bradford et al., 2004; El Sheikh et al., 2008; Harold et al., 2004; Shamir et al., 2005). For example, Bradford and colleagues (2004) found a link between inter-parental conflict and children's adjustment among school-going adolescents in Bangladesh, China, India, Bosnia, Germany, Palestine, Colombia, the United States and three ethnic groups within South Africa. A comparison between children from the US and Israel found children reacted negatively to marital conflict across cultures and were sensitive to the topics of conflict, whether or not it was escalating and whether or not conflict was resolved (Shamir, et al., 2005).

Some studies have reported differences in the strengths of pathways and there are suggestions that the impact of conflict via its influence on parenting is less applicable to Hispanic and African American children than to European American (e.g. Buehler and Gerard, 2002). However, some studies have not drawn similar conclusions about parenting pathways (e.g. Fauber et al., 1990; Gonzales et al., 2000; Lindahl et al., 2004; El-Sheikh et al 2008; Stutzman et al., 2011) and others have found more similarities than differences across different cultures (Tschann et al., 1999; Cummings et al., 2003).

Peer relations/social support

Although children's relationships with friends can suffer as a result of conflict between parents, for example, children may be more aggressive or lack the social skills they need to manage their friendships (Parke et al., 2001), there is also some evidence that friendships or a relationship with a supportive adult outside of the family can buffer children from the impact of a high conflict home (Wasserstein and La Greca, 1996; Rogers and Holmbeck, 1997; Criss et al., 2002). For example, one longitudinal study looking at family adversity, which included a measure of inter-parental conflict, followed 5 year old children over a 2 year period (Criss et al., 2002). They found that peer relationships reduced the likelihood of children exposed to family adversity (including conflict between parents) developing externalising difficulties. This protective effect held regardless of child gender, ethnicity, temperament or cognitive processing patterns (Criss et al., 2002). Another study found that for children exposed to discord between parents, a positive relationship with a sibling or an adult outside of the family (e.g., relative, teacher) protected children from psychological difficulties (Jenkins and Smith, 1990). However, there is little evidence that support seeking per se is a protective coping strategy in the face of conflict (Shelton and Harold, 2007). As with many of these moderators, more research is required to understand fully how these factors operate.

To summarise

- A range of factors explain why some children are more vulnerable to the impact of conflict between parents than others.
- Boys and girls may experience and react to conflict differently, although with equally deleterious outcomes for both. This is because of differences in how girls and boys react to conflict, socialisation into different roles and interactions between the sex of the parent and the sex of the child.
- Older children appear to be more vulnerable to the impact of conflict between parents than younger children. This may be explained by a number of factors, including: a failure to fully capture the impact on younger children; the interplay of age and developmental stage and how that affects children's response to conflict; or simply that older children have become more sensitive to conflict because they have been exposed to it for longer compared to younger children.
- Children's temperaments can also serve to increase or reduce their vulnerability to inter-parental conflict. Children with a difficult temperament are more vulnerable to the impact of conflict between parents.
- Children's coping strategies can also be important. In general, emotion-focused strategies, that help children to distance themselves from parental conflict, are associated with better outcomes for children than problem-solving strategies that may result in children becoming embroiled in the situation.
- Children's physiological makeup can also play an important role in differentiating between children who are at greater risk of poor developmental outcomes.

- A warm sibling relationship can buffer children from the impact of a high conflict home. However, sibling relationships can also suffer with complicated alliances and divisions emerging within families, or as one sibling protects him or herself by deflecting parental anger towards a sibling.
- Research has also focused on how family relationship patterns are passed from one generation to the next. One explanation is that conflict between parents disturbs other relationships within the family, such as between a parent and child. There is also evidence to suggest that a family environment marked by destructive conflict affects normal developmental processes, such as brain development, which in turn affect children's psychological development.
- Until recently it could be argued that shared genes could explain this 'intergenerational transmission' of troubled ways of relating. However, innovatively designed studies using samples of children and parents who are not genetically related provide evidence that this is not the case. Rather, family environmental factors such as inter-parental conflict and harsh parenting practices affect children's psychological development irrespective of whether or not parents and children are genetically related.

CHAPTER 6

REVIEW OF CONFLICT-BASED INTERVENTIONS FOR COUPLES

The previous chapters have examined the links between inter-parental conflict and children's adjustment. This evidence suggests that conflict between parents can have a negative impact on children's social, emotional and behavioural development. Understanding more about what elements of conflict are important and the factors which put children at risk of experiencing harmful effects are useful in considering how best to minimise the impact of destructive conflict behaviours on children, as well as exploring ways to prevent these patterns of behaviour from developing in the first place (Cummings and Davies, 2010).

This chapter explores the growing evidence base from various couple or family interventions which have covered areas relating to conflict. It outlines the impact these have on parental, child, and relationship wellbeing.

What should conflict interventions focus on?

Evidence suggests that it is not the presence of conflict per se which relates to child outcomes; it is the type of conflict behaviour demonstrated and the duration and intensity of the conflict which are important (Cummings and Davies, 2010).This indicates that focus in intervention programmes should be placed on raising parents' awareness of the effect of conflict on children and helping parents to develop the skills required to reduce destructive conflict.

Chapter 4 showed that inter-parental conflict can have an indirect effect on child wellbeing by affecting parenting and the parent–child relationship (Schoppe-Sullivan et al., 2007). Therefore, interventions may limit this potential 'spillover' effect, by promoting effective parenting skills. A more direct way in which children are influenced by inter-parental conflict is through their own interpretations and understanding of the conflict (Harold et al., 2007). Interventions which help children and young people to understand and cope with their feelings following inter-parental conflict may also be useful.

Chapter 5 identified various risk and protective (or resilience) factors which have been related to child responses to conflict (Cummings and Davies, 2010).These findings are useful in helping to target interventions at families who may be experiencing difficulties and where children could be at risk of future adjustment problems. The findings also help to highlight protective factors which can be promoted through interventions.

The extensive literature on inter-parental conflict does provide ideas for interventions in this area. However, a review of the wider family and couple intervention literature is needed to help explore the practical implications of how to effectively help families experiencing such conflict.

Are there effective conflict interventions?

The field of family interventions is complex. This chapter focuses mainly on preventive interventions with parents where the programme includes a component on the couple relationship and some reference to conflict and communication between couples.

The chapter is not an inclusive review of all available evidence, rather it summarises key findings in the area and identifies some promising approaches. It also attempts to promote discussion about future innovations. There is no direct discussion of clinical or therapeutic practice, as this mainly focuses on more entrenched conflict, which is beyond the scope of this publication. The same applies to programmes concerned with helping families cope with domestic violence (see Rivett et al., 2006). General parenting programmes for divorced families are not covered, although this chapter does focus on programmes which look particularly at helping parents cope with conflict during separation and divorce (see Goodman et al., 2004; Grych, 2005; and Sigal et al., 2011).

The interventions outlined in this chapter cover a range of different approaches, which vary in content and programme aims, including:

- Those improving parenting with an additional emphasis on enhancing couple relationships.
- Those taking a wider goal of improving general family functioning, particularly at times of key transitions, such as new parenthood.
- Those focusing specifically on aspects of conflict within the couple relationship (either for separating couples or those still in a relationship).

- Those which take an earlier preventative approach, by aiming to strengthen the couple relationship by providing general relationship education and training in interpersonal skills, before problems arise.

These interventions differ in their reach, with some providing a universal approach to a given population, whilst others are targeted at particular parents or couple groups. There is also variation across interventions in the type of outcomes reported and who these outcomes relate to. Key outcome areas include aspects of the couple relationship and parenting or parent–child relationship, as well as adult and child adjustment indicators. However, there are very few studies which report on outcomes across all these areas.

Finally, there is considerable range in the quality of the evaluation research used to assess the effectiveness of couple interventions. This review focuses on programmes which have been robustly evaluated (mainly those published since 2001), including, where available, the use of an equivalent control group and random allocation to intervention and control conditions, pre- and post-intervention measurement, and follow-up assessment. Where this level of design is sparse or in the process of being conducted, other literature is drawn on and the limitations of design are highlighted.

Focus on parenting: parent education programmes

Research suggests that parents engaged in a distressed couple relationship are typically also more hostile and aggressive toward their child and less sensitive and emotionally responsive to their needs (Erel and Burman, 1995). One implication of this is that parenting programmes which aim to enhance parenting skills and parent–child relationships could buffer children from the effects of parental conflict.

However, research suggests that good parent–child relationships are difficult to sustain in an atmosphere of conflict and are not sufficient to protect children from the effects of parental discord. Parenting programmes tend to be less successful with those parents who are in conflict as the conflict seems to undermine parents' ability to cooperate and engage with the programme (Webster-Stratton and Hammond, 1999).

This suggests that parent training programmes need to be broadened to emphasise aspects of the couple relationship, such as partner involvement and support, as well as communication, problem solving and coping skills.

Parenting intervention programmes that take account of the couple relationship

Including a component on the couple relationship in parent support programmes appears to offer some promise. Parents who received an ADVANCE version of the 'Incredible Years' parenting course, which included additional sessions on communication skills, problem solving, and personal self-control, experienced improvements in both marital communication and child problem-solving skills compared to parents in the BASIC training group. Furthermore, the children from the ADVANCE group showed greater pro-social solutions during a problem solving task (Webster-Stratton, 1994).

Results suggest that focusing on helping families to manage personal distress and interpersonal relationship issues significantly improves outcomes for families (Webster-Stratton and Reid, 2003).

More recent evidence indicates that a group-based approach to delivering couple focused content can be effective in improving outcomes for children, parents and the family as a whole. These effects also appear to be greater than interventions which focus on parenting aspects alone (Cowan et al., 2011).

In the 'School Children and their Families' project, Cowan, Cowan and colleagues randomly assigned 100 couples to a low-dose control condition or to one of two intervention conditions. These involved couples' group discussion meetings over 16 weeks that focused on either couple relationship issues or on parenting issues. Both intervention conditions showed positive improvements on parent–child relationships and children's adjustments to kindergarten and first grade. The groups focusing on the couple relationship also demonstrated additional benefits in their couple interaction quality, such as reduced conflict (Cowan et al., 2005).

Follow-up evaluations have shown that the advantages of participating in these groups persisted 6 and 10 years after the initial intervention, including higher marital satisfaction and greater children's adaptation to high school (Cowan et al., 2011). These findings indicate that a couple-based group intervention is effective and can have long-term effects on the family and child.

Programmes that focus on at-risk groups and challenging transitions

The above 'School Children and their Families' programme is based on a family systems model, which proposes that children's development is predicted by risks and buffers in areas such as the quality of the parent–child relationship and the quality of the relationship between the parents.

The family systems model underpins a number of other prevention-based family intervention programmes developed by Cowan, Cowan and colleagues, which target families who may be at risk of experiencing elevated conflict.

An adaptation of the family systems model was used in the 'Promoting Father's Engagement with Children' project (Cowan et al., 2007). This programme was aimed primarily at low-income Mexican American and European American families, based on the existing evidence that poverty creates conditions that exacerbate inter-parental and parent–child conflict. Having both partners involved in the intervention is believed to provide a greater opportunity for encouraging change between as well as within couples (Cowan et al., 2009). Both the 'Promoting Fathers Engagement' and the 'School Children and their Families' programmes were developed from an earlier couples intervention, originally created for new parents.

The transition to parenthood has been identified as one of the most challenging family transitions (Huston and Holmes, 2004). During this time, many parents show a decline in relationship satisfaction (Twenge et al., 2003; Mitnick et al., 2009) and positive couple communication (Cowan and Cowan, 2000; Pinquart and Teubert, 2010), as well as an increase in conflict (Glade et al., 2005). This suggests that interventions aimed at new parents should include some focus on couples' ability to manage conflict.

A number of interventions have been designed to help parents negotiate this period of change and to promote effective family functioning. Table 6.1 outlines some universal transition to parenting programmes that focus on improving couple relationships and which have been robustly evaluated in the past 10 years. The goal of many of these interventions is to strengthen couple relationships by preparing couples for the difficulties associated with becoming a parent and promoting relationship skills (e.g., communication, conflict management), mutual support, and realistic expectations about parenthood (Pinquart and Teubert, 2010).

In summary, all the transition to parenthood programmes outlined in Table 6.1 include a degree of content overlap, covering aspects such as: promoting couple communication, effective conflict management, realistic expectations, sharing of roles and responsibilities, couple intimacy, couple time, and promoting parenting sensitivity. However, these intervention programmes vary in two main ways: a) the length and intensity of the programme and, b) the process of learning applied (Petch and Halford, 2008). In terms of intensity of the programme, this ranged from the shortest being 1 hour of professional contact in the 'Marriage Moments' programme and the greatest being 24 weekly group meetings in the 'Becoming a Family' programme.

Although the measured outcomes and findings varied across these programmes, many demonstrate enhanced couple relationship satisfaction following intervention. Only the brief 'Marriage Moments' programme failed to enhance relationship satisfaction. Where programmes included behavioural skill training, improvements in couple communication were also demonstrated (Shapiro and Gottman, 2005; Halford et al., 2010). Despite these interventions targeting the transition to parenthood, only one study examined intervention effects on parenting. This showed that parents in both the mother-focused and couple psycho-education conditions reported low levels of parenting stress (Halford et al., 2010).

An earlier review of the evidence from interventions to assist new parents shows that the majority of programmes target either the couple relationship or parenting, with few programmes addressing both areas (Petch and Halford, 2008). It is recommended that more transition to parenthood interventions include partners and that both parenting and couple processes should be included in these programmes. A greater focus on skills training and more objective assessment of these outcomes is also suggested, rather than relying on parents' self-reports.

A recently conducted meta-analysis of 21 controlled couple-focused interventions with expectant and new parents (including 10 studies with randomisation since 2001) revealed that interventions had, on average, small but significant effects on couple communication, psychological wellbeing, and couple adjustment (Pinquart and Teubert, 2010). Stronger effects emerged if the intervention included more than five sessions, included an antenatal and postnatal component, and was led by trained professionals rather than semi-professionals.

Interventions that focus specifically on conflict

So far, this chapter has indicated that some parenting and family functioning programmes can help enhance elements of couple interactions, such as improving communication and reducing conflict. There are other interventions which take a more specific focus on reducing inter-parental conflict or preventing the harmful effects it may have. This includes giving parents information about conflict and its effects on children, whilst providing training in conflict and anger management, and promoting effective communication skills.

Where conflict is frequent, intense, child-related and poorly resolved, this is particularly upsetting for children of all ages. Conversely, where the conflict is expressed without animosity, is unrelated to the child and successfully

Table 6.1: Couple interventions which have focused on the transition to parenthood

Programme (Name and references)	Intervention details	Sample and methods	Findings
Becoming a Family Cowan & Cowan (2000) Schulz, Cowan & Cowan (2006)	Weekly group-support sessions for parents during the three months prior to and following the birth of their first child. Group sessions held with 4-5 couples and lasted 2.5 hours each session. Trained co-leaders introduced topics in each session and facilitated group discussion around these areas.	Couples expecting their first child were randomly assigned to an intervention (n= 28) condition or non-intervention comparison group (n=38). Most of the couples involved were married and described themselves as White or Caucasian. The mean age for men was 30.5 years and 29.2 for women.	Involvement in the support groups had a significant positive effect on the quality and stability of couple relationships for three years after the birth. Further analysis found that the intervention does not prevent divorce over the longer-term, but it does help to maintain satisfaction with the relationship for the majority of couples who stay together. This is compared to the normative significant decline in relationship satisfaction found in couples in the comparison group

Programme (Name and references)	Intervention details	Sample and methods	Findings
Bringing Baby Home Shapiro & Gottman (2005)	A psycho-communicative-educational 2-day couples' workshop. The workshop focuses on 3 goals: a) to strengthen the couple relationship and prepare new parents for marital difficulties associated with the transition to parenthood; b) facilitating fathers as well as mothers involvement in the family; c) giving basic information about infant psychological development. Workshops involved a combination of lectures, demonstrations, role plays, videos and communication exercises, such as building skills in coping with conflict and maintenance of friendship and intimacy.	Couples were eligible for the study if they were either expecting a baby or had a baby born within the last 3 months. 18 couples were randomly allocated to the intervention group to receive the 2-day couples' workshop, whilst 20 couples were assigned to a waiting list control trial. Couples were predominately white middle class.	The intervention was effective compared to the control group in maintaining relationship quality, preventing postpartum depression, and improving observed hostile affect. Interestingly, initial post-intervention levels of hostile affect during conflict seemed to increase for the intervention group. However, at a one-year follow up, marital hostility in both husbands and wives was significantly lower in the workshop than the control group.

Programme (Name and references)	Intervention details	Sample and methods	Findings
Couple CARE for Parents (CCP) Halford, Petch & Creedy (2010)	Focuses on the promotion of positive couple adjustment to parenthood via skill-training in key relationship areas (including couple communication, conflict management and partner support). The programme consists of a face-to-face workshop (involving couple activities, presentations, video demonstrations and group skill training), two home visits and three self-directed sessions (involving watching a short DVD, completing exercises and having a brief telephone conversation with the CCP educator).	80 couples were randomly allocated to receive either the CCP or the 'Becoming a Parent' (BAP) programme. The latter, was provided to the mother only and did not include the specific skill-training or couple relationship focus as found in the CCP, but both programmes did include the same infant care information.	Relative to those who received the BAP program, couples in the CCP condition demonstrated reduced negative couple communication and prevented the negative erosion of relationship satisfaction in women but not men. No significant difference in level of parenting stress between the programmes. Follow-up assessment indicated a slight reduction of CCP effects on couple communication a year later.

Programme (Name and references)	Intervention details	Sample and methods	Findings
Marriage Moments Hawkins, Fawcett, Carroll & Gilliland (2006)	Self-directed low-intensity programme which emphasises strengthening the couple relationship. Addition of relationship-based components to existing antenatal classes. For 5 weeks couples are provided with a short video and in-class activity for 15 minutes at the end of their classes. Also provided with an activity workbook to guide active learning at home.	155 married couples expecting their first child were recruited and randomly allocated to either a instructor-encouraged (n = 51) or self-guided (n= 55) treatment group; or to a non-treatment control group.	Treatment groups (both instructor-encouraged and self-directed conditions) were no better off at the end of the study than the control group in terms of marital quality and satisfaction, or adjustment to the transition to parenthood. Suggested reasons for the lack of intervention effects include the low dosage and lack of skills component.

Programme (Name and references)	Intervention details	Sample and methods	Findings
Family Foundations Feinberg & Kan (2008) Feinberg, Jones, Kan & Goslin (2010)	8 interactive psycho-educational, skills based group classes (groups of 6-10 couples). 4 prenatal and 4 postnatal sessions. Focus on enhancing coparenting relationship (the ways parents coordinate parenting, support one another and manage conflict regarding childrearing). Control group: Couples mailed a brochure about selecting quality child care.	169 couples expecting first child and were living together (regardless of marital status). 82% of participants were married and majority were White. Mean age of mothers was 28 and 30 for fathers. After pre-test measures couples were randomly assigned to intervention (n=89) or no-treatment control conditions (n= 80). Post-test data collected when babies were approximately 6 months old and follow-up data collected three years post-birth.	Both intervention mothers and fathers reported better coparental support than those in the control condition. Fathers in the intervention group also reported greater parenting-based closeness with their partners, whilst mothers in this group had lower levels of anxiety and depression when compared to the control group. Intervention parents showed less difficulty in the parent–child relationship. However, there was no significant program effect on co-parenting undermining. At 3 year follow-up, intervention parents reported less parental stress, more parental efficacy, less depression, and better coparenting quality than control parents. Children in the intervention families also demonstrated better social competency.

resolved, children learn valuable lessons about dealing with conflict they may apply to their own lives (Harold and Murch, 2005).

The following sections look at interventions which deal more specifically with aspects of inter-parental conflict, including those targeted on separated or divorced couples, and a promising programme which deals with conflict among couples who are still together.

Couples who have separated/divorced

Research evidence suggests that children's adjustment after separation and divorce is strongly related to the level and type of conflict between their parents, both before and after separation, as well as the quality of the relationship they have with both their mother and father (Sigal et al., 2011). Existing marital conflict literature provides important insights into how, why and when conflict between separated parents adversely affects children (Harold and Murch, 2005).

Couples who are in the midst of divorce or separation may be more likely to use destructive forms of conflict behaviour. As separated parents are still bound together by the child, it is not surprising that the topic of their conflict is often related to the child. Conflicts where children are put, or made to feel, 'in the middle' of their parents' conflicts are particularly problematic. Children's appraisal of their parents' conflict appears to play an important role in their adjustment, particularly when they blame themselves or feel responsible for their parents' marital arguments (Harold and Leve, 2012).

There are a number of interventions developed for separated and divorced parents to improve outcomes for both parents and children. Most families who require assistance in negotiating the divorce process respond to low-intensity interventions. Universal prevention-based programmes are considered appropriate for separated parents, unless there are indicators that a more targeted treatment is needed, such as where more entrenched conflict is evident (McIntosh and Deacon-Wood, 2003). Early prevention programmes commonly include both an educational/informational component and one which addresses feelings and skills.

Research suggests that prevention programmes for separated parents will be most effective in promoting children's adaptation to divorce if they can reduce the levels of destructive conflict that children are exposed to, foster good parent–child relationships, and keep children from being caught in the middle of parental conflict (Grych, 2005). There are several programmes for separated parents which focus particularly on inter-parental conflict. Table 6.2 includes some of these programmes which have been evaluated.

A recent review of parenting education programmes for separating and divorcing parents identified research design limitations of many of the existing evaluations (Sigal et al., 2011). Although a few programmes seem to indicate some promise, there is a need for more robust assessment of programme effects. Brief, generic educational programmes alone, even skills-based programmes, may not be enough to make a substantial difference in post-divorce family life for children. Rather, these programmes may have indirect and possibly cumulative influences on expectations and attitudes regarding the appropriate control of parental conflict for the sake of children.

The review does give an indication of what more effective programmes commonly include, such as: a) educating parents about the impact of high quality parenting and low inter-parental conflict; b) a component to build motivation to strengthen the quality of parenting and not undermine the other parent; and c) an active skill-building component including modelling, role play and feedback (Sigal et al., 2011).

Evidence suggests that the impact of separation and divorce on children may be determined more by the level of conflict that exists between parents before, during and after the breakdown of the parental relationship than the actual breakdown itself (Harold and Murch, 2005). This suggests that a focus for earlier prevention on improving conflict behaviours before significant problems arise would be beneficial.

Couples who are still together

A recent addition in this field has been the development of a prevention-based programme for couples which specifically builds on the empirical research into inter-parental conflict and child outcomes (Cummings and Davies, 2010). Cummings and colleagues have developed a psycho-educational (awareness raising and skills building) programme which aims to teach couples better ways to handle their conflicts before serious problems develop. This focuses on replacing destructive ways of expressing conflict with more constructive behaviours.

Early findings showed that a single session was effective in improving parents' knowledge about marital conflict. Couples in the treatment group also displayed less hostility in front of their children and showed improvements in conflict tactics following the programme, compared with pre-programme levels (Faircloth and Cummings, 2008; also see Cummings and Davies, 2010). However, limitations in the research design in terms of a small sample size, the possibility of placebo effects with the waiting list control, reliance on self-report, and the absence of random allocation, means that the implications of these findings are limited.

A further study addressed many of these concerns to demonstrate that a brief, four session psycho-educational programme, 'Happy Couples and Happy Kids' (HCHK), can help couples from community samples manage marital conflict better (Cummings et al., 2008). Following facilitator led presentations, couples were given written, take-home definitions of the behaviours discussed in the session. Video clips portraying these conflict behaviours were also presented. Parents were shown scenarios about everyday themes of marital conflict either between couples alone or between couples with a child present. Group discussions were used to help couples identify and understand the implications of the conflict behaviours and to consider what the actors could have done to handle the situation differently. Additional weekly communication training sessions were also included in the programme.

Couples with children between 4 and 8 years of age were randomly assigned to one of three conditions: a) a parent-only group (n= 24); b) a parent–child group (n=33); or c) a self-study group (n=33) as a comparison group. More constructive and less destructive marital conflict was observed in the treatment groups, compared to the control group. Parents changed their interaction with partners in conflict situations. Parents were more supportive of their partners, more emotionally positive during interactions, and more likely to move toward a resolution. These changes were also linked with improvements in other family processes, such as improved marital satisfaction, and

Table 6.2: Conflict focused interventions for separated parents

Programme (Name and references)	Intervention details	Sample and methods	Findings
The Children in the Middle Kramer et al. (1998)	1 Face-to-face session, three hour programme that focuses on reducing children's exposure to destructive conflict and preventing them from being caught in the middle of their parents' disputes. This programme emphasises directly teaching skills for resolving conflict and keeping children out of the middle of parental disagreements, via behavioural modelling techniques. More recently, the programme has been adapted to an online format. There are currently plans to robustly evaluate this approach and to compare outcomes with the traditional face-to-face delivery.	Study compared effectiveness of an information-based divorce programme with the skills orientated Children in the Middle intervention. Another no intervention group formed a control group. A follow-up was conducted 3 months after the interventions.	Neither program had effects on occurrence of parental conflict over child issues. However both divorce programmes reduced child exposure to parental conflict. The Children in the Middle programme showed a significantly greater impact on parents' communication skills.

Programmme (Name and references)	Intervention details	Sample and methods	Findings
Kids in Divorce and Separation Program (K.I.D.S) Shifflett & Cummings (1999)	Seeks to help parents improve their management of conflict and inform them about the impact of divorce on children.	Evidence of effectiveness was derived from a random allocation to receive the programme (n=17), a wait-list group (n=10) and a control group recruited from an existing parenting class (n=12).	Participants in the first trial of the programme demonstrated an increased knowledge about conflict/divorce issues and a decrease in parental-reported destructive conflict behaviour. The changes were maintained at one month (albeit a short follow-up interval) after the programme.
Kids Turn Cookston & Fung (2011)	This is a community-based programme which includes 6 sessions designed to be offered to all members of the divorcing family, with parents in different rooms of mixed-sex participants and children in separated, age-appropriate groups.	61 parents with children between 4 and 17 took part in the programme. The majority of parents were female, and aged between 25-60, with an average age of 41. This study did lack any random allocation and comparison to an equivalent control group, but is included here because of the programme focus on interparental conflict.	Improvements over time in inter-parental conflict, the number of topics parents argue about, parental alienation behaviours parent anxiety and depression, and children's internalising behaviours.

Programmme (Name and references)	Intervention details	Sample and methods	Findings
Dads for Life Cookston, Braver, Griffin, De Luse & Miles (2006)	Working with fathers to improve the father-child relationship and increase fathers' parenting skills. Included 8 group sessions lasting 1 hour and 45 minutes and two 45 minutes sessions. Of all sessions, half were devoted to the parent–child relationship. The other half of the programme was devoted to reducing inter-parental conflict.	Eligibility criteria: Couple divorced in past 4-10 months; At least one child between 4-12; Mother had primary custody of the child (as the programme was aimed at fathers who did not have primary custody). 214 fathers were randomly allocated to either the intervention condition (n= 127) or a control group (n=87), who received two self-help books related to the subject matter. Both mothers and fathers were assessed at 4 time points: Before random assignment; Immediately after the programme; 4 months after the programme; 1 year after the programme	Following fathers' involvement in the programme both mothers and fathers reported less conflict compared to those in the control condition.

Programmme (Name and references)	Intervention details	Sample and methods	Findings
The Collaborative Divorce Project (CDP) Pruett, Insabella & Gustafson (2005)	A more intensive programme that is voluntary and court-based for families with children 6 years and younger. The intervention is made up of 7 different components: introduction to the legal system; 2 session educational series with interactive activities, skill building and discussion to concentrate on key issues such as conflict resolution; a feedback session and consultation on parenting plan development; therapeutic-focused mediation sessions; intensive education for higher conflict families; conflict resolution meetings with attorneys and follow-up sessions 9 months after implementation.	Families with a child aged 6 or younger were recruited from two US court districts upon filing for divorce or court action. 161 families were randomly assigned to either the CDP intervention condition or a waiting list control group. Parents were primarily Caucasian.	Parents in the intervention group reported less parental distress and conflict, greater use of alternative means of dispute resolution (non-litigation), more father involvement and payment of child support, and better cognitive and behavioural functioning in children. The primary impact of the intervention for both parents was believed to be through reduced parental conflict.

parenting and child adjustment. Changes in knowledge over time were also linked with changes in conflict behaviours, suggesting that knowledge may be an important factor in behavioural change.

The programme appeared to have less initial impact on more complex constructive behaviours, such as problem solving. Greater time, practice and mastery of these more complex skills may be needed before having an impact on behavioural change (Cummings et al., 2008). More recently, evidence from a 2-year follow-up assessment showed that both treatment groups demonstrated greater knowledge about the effects of conflict and displayed behavioural improvements in constructive conflict, including problem solving behaviours (Faircloth et al., 2011). These findings support the long-term efficacy of this programme and suggest that a psycho-educational intervention can help to prevent problems associated with marital conflict.

Early intervention: relationship preparation or enhancement courses

Research findings show that couples can establish styles of conflict early on in their relationship and these patterns tend to remain stable during the relationship (Gottman, 1994). The work outlined above suggests that conflict training can be effective for couples already with children or those preparing to be parents, but what about intervening even earlier? Is couple conflict training any more successful when offered to couples at the start of their relationship?

There are some couple relationship education programmes which seek to take an early prevention approach by enhancing the quality of couple relationships and building on key inter-relational skills, before relationship problems develop. These programmes are targeted at couples in committed relationships, including those who are engaged, newly married, or who cohabit (Halford, 2004). Couple Relationship Education (CRE) is the provision of structured education to couples about relationship knowledge, attitudes and skills (Hawkins et al., 2004; Halford et al., 2008).

Although there are a number of relationship skills-based programmes which have been developed, few have been robustly tested. One such programme which has been extensively evaluated is the Prevention and Relationship Enhancement Programme – PREP (Halford et al., 2008). PREP includes a key focus on destructive conflict; it teaches couples how to identify and limit destructive patterns of behaviour, learn how to manage conflict well, and to promote intimacy. Couples who took part in trials of PREP showed some improvements on measures of conflict management and communication compared with couples who did not take part. However these differences tended to diminish over time (Knutson and Olson, 2003).

Findings from meta-analyses indicate that, although relationship education offers some potential for improved relationship outcomes, there is room for improvement. In particular, couples may need more help in utilising their new skills in their day-to-day communication challenges (Carroll and Doherty, 2003; Fawcett et al., 2010).

The use of self-regulation has been recommended as one way to assist long-term maintenance of adaptive relationship behaviours. However, findings suggest that the outcome of such an approach may be influenced by initial risk level (Halford et al., 2001). One implication is that relationship education may be best targeted at couples considered high risk for relationship problems. However, these programmes have traditionally reached only a minority of couples (usually middle-income, married couples, and those already reasonably satisfied with their relationship). Couples with certain relationship risk factors tend to be underrepresented in such programmes (Halford et al., 2006).

There is a need for a more flexible and innovative approach to relationship education. There have been some efforts to explore the effects of relationship education for low-income and at-risk communities (Halford, 2004; Ooms and Wilson, 2004). There have also been attempts to find new ways of delivering these programmes as an alternative to face-to-face methods. For example, self-directed methods such as web-based sources have been found to have comparable effects to a traditional group workshop format (Duncan et al., 2009).

Finally, early relationship education programmes tend to cover a range of couple interactions, rather than focusing specifically on conflict behaviours (however there is often reference to couple communication). This has meant that many reported outcomes have focused on the quality, satisfaction or stability of couple relationships, rather than particular conflict behaviours. The current review suggests that management of conflict is of particular relevance for child wellbeing. As early relationship education traditionally focused largely on engaged or newly married couples without children, there has been little exploration as to whether this early intervention impacts on later inter-parental conflict management. It is also important to acknowledge the change in family structure (see Harold and Leve, 2012). Significant numbers of children are now born outside of marriage, suggesting that early relationship education should also be focused at other stages, such as the transition to parenthood. Also, Lavner and Bradbury (2012) suggest that negative interactions and patterns of conflict may only arise in later stages of relationships, even among 'satisfied newly-weds', which may pose a challenge to address such matters early on in a relationship.

What does the current evidence tell us?

In summary, the above evidence provides a comprehensive review of some of the relationship interventions which have included a reference to couple or inter-parental conflict. These range from programmes focused on parenting and including an additional relationship component, those targeted at key transitional times such as becoming parents for the first time, programmes with a more centred approach to dealing with inter-parental conflict (including for separated and intact couples), and preventive or early intervention approaches to relationship education.

Although the specific level of focus on conflict and the stage of intervention vary across programmes, a common finding is that couple-based programmes, which include content that addresses conflict, do have some measurable improvements in the couple relationship domain. Where skills-based training is included, improvements in communication and couple interaction are commonly reported. The conflict literature identifies ways in which inter-parental conflict can negatively impact on children. By improving the couple relationship and minimising destructive conflict, this may have better outcomes for children. However, there are still few studies which report directly on outcomes of couple-based interventions for children.

The following chapter looks at implications from this review of existing interventions to help identify when it is best to intervene, with whom, and what are the most effective ways of doing so, as well as what further research is needed to advance intervention practice further.

To summarise

- Intervention programmes which focus on couple interaction can help to prevent the potential 'spillover' effect of inter-parental conflict on children.
- Interventions which cover couple related issues as well as parenting issues are more effective in improving outcomes for children, parents, and the family as a whole; compared with those which deal with parenting issues alone.
- These interventions can be targeted at couples who are at increased risk of experiencing conflict, such as new or expectant parents, as well as those who may already be experiencing conflict.
- Another approach is to focus on providing relationship education to couples at an earlier stage in their relationship, before conflict problems arise.
- Where programmes include behavioural skill training, improvements in couple communication are found as well as enhanced relationship satisfaction.
- Awareness raising and skills training in specific conflict related areas is linked to a reduction in destructive, and an increase in constructive, conflict behaviours.
- More support may be needed for couples to apply the skills learnt to everyday settings, especially for those in deprived circumstances or experiencing more complex difficulties.

CHAPTER 7

IMPLICATIONS FOR PRACTICE: HOW TO HELP FAMILIES

This chapter explores the implications of the findings presented in the last chapter on couple interventions. It aims to highlight what this means for those working with families in trying to help parents manage their conflict and avoid its potentially harmful influence on children. The limitations of current intervention research and new innovative ideas for dealing with inter-parental conflict are also highlighted in this chapter.

When should we intervene?

Early intervention is believed to offer benefits in long-term outcomes and is considered to be more effective than treatment-based interventions, which are provided once problems arise (Rutter, 2010). Many of the programmes presented in the last chapter focus on a prevention-based approach by identifying couples and families who may be at risk of experiencing higher stress and couple disagreement, rather than those who are already characterised by entrenched levels of conflict. Even the programmes aimed at separated and divorced parents predominately target those with a more normative and less extreme conflict style (McIntosh and Deacon-Wood, 2003). It is widely recognised that behaviour change is greater and more sustainable with earlier intervention, rather than trying to change ingrained and longstanding patterns of interaction (Dolan et al., 2010).

Early intervention is important, but how early is early enough?

The evidence from relationship education or preparation programmes indicates that couple interventions have traditionally been applied to couples entering marriage. Entry to marriage represents a key time for intervention as some couples may face significant challenges as they adapt to the changes and new commitment in their relationship. However, for many couples, marriage may not represent the beginning of a relationship in the same way as it did in the past. The majority of couples now cohabit before marriage and a growing number also have a child or children outside of marriage (Hunt, 2009; Lloyd and Lacey, 2012). These changes in relationship formation mean that interventions are also offered during other transition points and life course changes, such as the transition to parenthood.

A diverse and flexible approach of when to target relationship intervention may be best in order to reach couples when they are more receptive to help and support, and perhaps more motivated to change behaviours if necessary (Halford, 2004; Hawkins et al., 2004; Cowan et al., 2010). Meanwhile, a useful time to target much earlier relationship education may be in preparing young people for future relationships (Halford, 2004). Research has found that a relationship education programme delivered to young adults helped to improve their conflict resolution skills, and resulted in more openness to involvement in later education programmes to strengthen couple relationships (Gardner, 2001). Changing destructive conflict behaviour and promoting effective communication and conflict resolution at this earlier stage could possibly have a longer term and more sustainable impact on future couple and family functioning. However, robust research over a long period of time is needed to test this fully.

Who should interventions focus on?

Couple intervention programmes which cover aspects of communication and conflict vary in their particular focus and in whom they directly involve. Most work solely with the couples themselves, many of whom are parents or soon to be parents; there are few which involve working with both parents and children.

In view of the importance of how children understand and respond to conflict (Harold and Murch, 2005), this lack of interventions directed at, or which involve children seems surprising. This may be because working with parents to deal with the causes of adjustment problems is more promising than working with children to find ways to buffer them from the effects of conflict. Parents have a better chance of changing their couple and parenting behaviours than children have of influencing their parents. Children, in reality, have little or no control over sources of adversity and, moreover, their abilities for coping are limited in relation to adults. But if parents are not in a position to modify their behaviour, or if relationship breakdown has already occurred, children need help to cope with their situation.

Even though parents bear primary responsibility for managing post-divorce conflict, programmes for children may be useful, particularly if they help children to develop skills for coping with situations where they may be caught up in inter-parental conflict (Grych, 2005). Children's programmes are not as widespread as parent-focused programmes, and concentrate mostly on school-age children (Pedro-Carroll, 2005). Sometimes these child interventions can form part of a programme that also includes a group for parents (Wolchik et al., 2000), or are delivered through school-based groups (Pedro-Carroll, 1997). Evidence regarding the effectiveness of child focused or dual parent and child focused programmes are currently inconclusive and more research in this area is needed (Grych, 2005).

On a more general level, there is a need to balance the provision of universal prevention programmes available to all interested individuals with the requirement for selective programmes designed to serve more at-risk or distressed individuals (Blanchard et al., 2009). The question of what is meant by 'at risk' and for what constitutes the risk is also important. Some programmes have targeted those who are considered to be at increased risk of experiencing inter-parental conflict, relationship breakdown, or other relationship difficulties, based on a combination of various personal, historical and contextual factors. These interventions may be most effective when tailored so that the content addresses issues that are relevant to the couples targeted (Halford et al., 2008). For example, targeted programmes to tackle parental substance abuse could benefit from an additional component which aims to reduce heightened inter-parental conflict (Fals-Stewart et al., 2004). Couples therapy for drug-abusing parents, which included elements relating to conflict, was shown to significantly improve children's psychosocial adjustment relative to families who did not take part in the couples' therapy sessions (Kelley and Fals-Stewart, 2002).

What are some common components of couple interventions?

The couple-based programmes reviewed earlier vary in several ways, including: when and for whom these interventions are targeted, curriculum content, and particular focus on conflict. There is also considerable range in the duration and intensity of these programmes, as well as how they are delivered and by whom. Some of these areas are covered later in considering what factors seem to influence intervention outcomes. However, there are also some common components between the programmes reviewed in the last chapter, which may help to address inter-parental conflict.

The use of groups

The use of a group framework to deliver programme content to several couples (or individuals in the case of separated parents) is evident in many of the interventions covered earlier. This offers a more cost-effective programme delivery than intensive one-to-one programmes. These programmes do tend to vary in the size of groups used and how they are run, with some opting for a classroom or workshop-based approach, where leaders run through the programme and teach relevant skills. Others use more group-based discussions, role plays, and exercises to cover related issues.

It is thought that the power of group intervention lies in participants discovering they are not alone and by sharing and learning from others' experiences (Cowan et al., 2010).

Being able to recognise that their experiences were not unusual seems to reduce the tendency for new parents to blame themselves or their partners for the stresses they were experiencing (Schulz et al., 2006). However, there has been little research which has explored what the specific group mechanisms are that impact on conflict outcomes. Similarly, more research is needed to explore what size group and type of group delivery is most effective.

It is important to note that some individuals or couples may be reluctant or even resistant to joining group-based interventions. The greater anonymity, flexibility and accessibility offered by self-administered or on-line programmes may appeal as an alternative. These innovative ways of delivering interventions are considered later in this chapter.

Awareness raising

Awareness raising focuses on the transmission of information, clarification of expectations, and increasing couples' understanding of key relationship processes that influence relationship outcomes (Halford, 2004). Many of the interventions covered earlier raise couples' awareness and understanding about issues which can affect their relationship, such as conflict and how it is dealt with. When targeted at parents, these interventions often cover the impact that inter-parental conflict can have on parenting and child outcomes. Conflict specific interventions also help parents to understand the difference between destructive and constructive conflict behaviours.

However, many of the couple-based interventions go beyond simply raising awareness by including a skills component in an attempt to improve outcomes for parents and children.

Skills training

Skills training refers to identifying key interpersonal skills to help couples improve and strengthen their relationship. Commonly, this includes helping couples to communicate more effectively (using skills such as active listening) and in some programmes this covers skills specifically relating to inter-parental conflict (such as conflict resolution, problem solving, etc.). The skills-based approach to intervention usually involves modelling, rehearsal, and feedback of skills, as well as activities promoting beliefs and attitudes associated with healthy relationships (Halford et al., 2008). These skills components follow behavioural modelling principles (see Taylor et al., 2005).

Behaviour modelling training (BMT) uses visual demonstrations of behaviours to promote knowledge and skills acquisition and improvement in attitudes, intentions and self-efficacy. BMT applies the principles of Bandura's (1977) Social Learning Theory to a learning environment, whereby, a change in belief about one's ability to successfully execute a given behaviour will mediate the demonstrated behaviour and the initiation and maintenance of that behaviour. Enhanced knowledge, self-efficacy, motivation and practice bolster imitative, and vicarious learning (Pidd, 2004).

Social Learning Theory has four core components described as attentional, retentional, reproduction and motivational. Essentially, BMT programmes involve the provision of information, an outline of the skills to be acquired, modelling of these skills including setting goals to use particular skills, practice, and implementation in 'real-life' followed by feedback.

Additional aspects of the BMT approach highlighted by Taylor et al. (2005) include the importance of distinguishing and labelling behaviours, the sequencing of behaviours from the least to most difficult, and the ability to rehearse scenarios that users develop themselves. In addition, they cite the work of Baldwin (1992) who argues that a mixture of positive and negative models (as opposed to positive only) is effective due to the greater stimulus variability (which is associated with generalisation) and the ability for people to 'unlearn' undesirable behaviours.

From a meta-analysis of 117 published and unpublished studies (a total of 279 effect sizes) of adult training programmes that used BMT, Taylor et al. (2005) conclude that BMT is an effective, psychologically based training intervention that has been used to produce sustainable improvements in a diverse range of skills (p.706). Compelling evidence to support the use of BMT approaches for improving family conflicts is provided by a recently evaluated Interactive Multi-Media programme using BMT, which targeted stepfamilies and parents of children aged 11-15 years.

From a randomised controlled trial, involving an intervention and delayed access control group, Gelatt et al. (2010) conclude that relatively brief exposure (a minimum of three weekly visits) to this online behavioural step-parent training programme had a positive impact on family and parenting functioning (such as family adjustment, life satisfaction and parent–child conflict), compared with step-parents who had not completed the course. A 60-day follow-up also indicated that the course improved aspects of the couple relationship (increased efficacy and intentions in shared parenting, and fewer relationship difficulties) and parenting (increased efficacy/confidence in parenting and a reduction in lax parenting practices). The authors conclude that the online BMT approach provides 'an effective family life education delivery mechanism' (p.581).

Many of the skills-based couple interventions identified in the previous chapter include BMT elements such as identifying negative behaviours and some form of modelling desired behaviours, via role play or video clips. Reviews of various couple interventions suggest that an active skills building component is important for programmes designed both for new parents (Petch and Halford, 2008) as well as those designed for separated parents (Sigal et al., 2011). Currently there appears to be little research which directly compares skills-based approaches with alternative methods, particularly in relation to conflict-based outcomes. However, recent evidence suggests that skills training in relationship education programmes does have additional benefits for couples beyond assessment and feedback, including greater couple communication and relationship satisfaction (Halford et al., 2010).

Results suggest that couples are capable of displaying learned improved communication behaviour in specific problem-solving exercises. Less clear, however, is whether couples incorporate those skills effectively into their everyday lives and during their disagreements (Hawkins et al., 2008; Blanchard et al., 2009).

Some argue that there are limitations to what skills-based interventions can achieve, particularly for at-risk and low-income communities. Whilst some couples may benefit from relationship skills alone, others will need relationship training and other supportive services (such as job assistance, financial counselling and substance abuse treatment). For couples who live in challenging environments, increased environmental and economic stress may interfere with their ability to learn and practice intervention skills (Bradbury and Karney, 2004). Targeting these stressful areas as part of the programme may be most effective. For other couples, relationship skills will not be appropriate at all; if there is evidence of domestic violence, for example (Ooms and Wilson, 2004).

Some researchers have argued that skills training and positive affect (the way couples display affection) interact with one another to influence programme outcomes (Bradbury and Karney, 2004; Bradbury and Lavner, 2012). It has been suggested that rather than focusing on changing negative aspects of couple relationships, more effort should be made to help couples to see ways of improving and maintaining positive aspects of their relationship (Glade et al., 2005). However, note how this is contradicted by a recent study by Lavner and Bradbury (2012) that stressed the importance of targeting negative communication patterns in relationships.

There is also noteworthy evidence from the US-based Supporting Healthy Marriage evaluation, launched in 2003 and recently reported in 2012 (Hsueh et al., 2012). This skills-based relationship education programme is designed to help low-income married couples strengthen their relationships. Reporting on the 12-month impact, programme participants (relative to a control condition) showed greater levels of marital happiness, lower levels of psychological distress and, especially pertinent to this review, less psychological and physical abuse from their partners.

In detailing the conceptual framework for the Supporting Healthy Marriage, the role of conflict is central. Alongside more 'positive appraisals of marital quality', the programme focuses on skills to foster 'more positive emotions and behaviours in interactions' (such as effective conflict resolution skills) and 'fewer negative emotions and behaviours in interactions' (such as fewer antagonistic or hostile behaviours). These skills are delivered in small group workshops and focus on decreasing negative interactions (including conflict management), increasing supportive interactions (e.g. by sharing time together), and managing stressful circumstances. The skills are delivered in a variety of ways including presentations, group discussions, group and couple activities, videos, and time for reflection.

Moderating factors

Currently there is some evidence beyond the general effectiveness of couple-based interventions, that attempts to explore what aspects affect outcomes and who may benefit most from such programmes (Wadsworth and Markman, 2012). Some of the factors which have been considered include: programme content and fidelity; dosage or duration of the intervention; programme engagement; and initial levels of risk of those involved in the intervention. Other factors that have also been raised are how training is delivered and by whom.

Programme content and fidelity

Various meta-analyses and reviews reveal that the content of interventions influence the outcomes of these programmes. For example, parenting programmes which include a couple component are more likely to report positive outcomes in the couple dynamic (Cowan et al., 2010), whilst improvements in aspects of couple communication are more likely to be found when the intervention includes specific skills training for these behaviours (Blanchard et al., 2009; Hawkins et al., 2008). In terms of conflict specific outcomes, it appears that couple interventions need to include a component which deals directly with inter-parental conflict (Cummings et al., 2008).

Related to programme content is the issue of programme fidelity. That is, how well do different trainers or facilitators stick to the original content and design of the intervention. Some couple interventions are highly structured with clear content and delivery guidelines. Others, however, rely more on the skill of the trainer to shape the intervention to the specific needs of particular groups, whilst still covering the key components or issues which form the intervention (Schulz et al., 2006). The outcomes of the latter may be more susceptible to differences in the ability and confidence of the trainers, as well as variations in group dynamics. This has implications for who delivers training and in what format for specific groups (which is covered in more detail below).

Dosage/duration

Dosage is an important part of any intervention: too little means ineffective treatment but too much can be costly (Hawkins et al., 2004). A meta-analysis of Relationship Education Programmes reveals that studies with moderate-dosage programmes (9-20 hours) have substantially larger effect sizes than low-dosage programmes (1-8 hour). There are few programmes assessing the impact of higher dosage programmes (21 hours+) (Hawkins et al., 2008). However, the level of dosage required for particular outcome effects does appear to vary. Whilst researchers found no further positive effect of relationship education on marriage satisfaction after about 20 hours, for decreasing conflict, this was only approximately 10 hours (Stanley et al., 2006).

Moderate dosages of couple intervention may be necessary to generate desired effects, at least for some couples. However, the effects of programme intensity may be related to other areas such as programme content;

awareness-based programmes are generally shorter than skills-training programmes. Additionally, dosage may be influenced by who the intervention is targeted at; a universal moderate dose programme may be sufficient for many couples, but those who are at greater risk of relationship distress or experiencing more entrenched conflict may need something more intense and targeted to their needs. This suggests that a flexible approach to couple relationship intervention is needed, where the dosage varies along a continuum of intensity (Hawkins et al., 2004).

Programme engagement

Programme engagement represents an individual's level of involvement in an intervention (Brown et al., 2011). Both individual and couple factors predict engagement in relationship interventions. Research findings indicate that marital status is the most powerful predictor of engagement in relationship education. Other areas such as gender, education, income and age are also important (Brown et al., 2011).

Providing individuals with the opportunity to engage is critical. People who have greater need for conflict intervention, due to various risk factors, may benefit from more engagement. However, those with greater need may also face greater barriers, such as: transportation difficulties; additional life stressors that distract them from taking part in such programmes; or pessimistic attitudes which undermine motivation to change.

Who the programme is targeted at: initial levels of risk

Relationship education interventions and parenting programmes tend to attract more parents from socioeconomically advantaged groups. Many research studies involve samples of white middle-class couples, often with above average education (Carroll and Doherty, 2003; Fawcett et al., 2010). The lack of racial/ethnic and economic diversity prevents reliable conclusions about the effectiveness of interventions for disadvantaged couples (Hawkins et al., 2008). The exception to this is the Supporting Healthy Marriage intervention noted above, which specifically targeted low-income couples (Hsueh et al., 2012).

Research suggests that outcomes of relationship-based interventions are influenced by risk level. Some studies suggest that high-risk couples benefit from skills-based relationship education compared with low-risk couples (Halford et al., 2001), whilst a meta-analysis indicates that longer-term programme effects are generally stronger for well-functioning couples (Blanchard et al., 2009).

Provision of training

Other factors which have recently been considered with regards to relationship intervention outcomes include: a) variations in programme delivery, comparing more traditional face-to-face measures with various self-assisted and online programmes; and b) differences in who the training or programme is provided by, comparing professional delivery with para-professional or volunteer involvement. Although the research evidence in these areas is largely provisional, both of these aspects involve important implications in terms of cost-effectiveness.

Consequently, there has been some focus in finding ways of delivering relationship-based interventions to more people but for reduced costs, whilst maintaining outcomes.

Innovative ideas for conflict intervention

There is limited information available, as yet, about whether variations in curriculum content, dosage (optimal length of intervention), and engagement, might affect conflict intervention. Still more exploration is also needed to know whether specific intervention variations might have stronger effects for different types of couples.

Most of these areas are directly relevant to issues of cost of interventions, which is particularly important at a time of reduced government funding (Cowan et al., 2010). So far, there are no published per-family cost estimates for various relationship-based interventions. There is a need to establish whether interventions can achieve comparable outcomes for reduced costs, whilst reaching more people. This includes reaching out to different groups, providing less highly trained professional engagement, and looking at alternative methods of delivery, rather than relying on more costly face-to-face engagement. These issues are outlined below.

Developing a community approach

Traditionally, attendance on relationship-based interventions has been over-represented by educated, middle-class, and low-conflict couples. More recently, there have been attempts to broaden the reach of these interventions by specifically targeting some high-risk couples through tailoring existing couple-relationship interventions and adopting a community-based approach (Rutter, 2010;

Cowan et al., 2010). Some examples of ways to engage with couples at higher risk of relationship problems, and encourage their involvement in relationship-based intervention programmes, are outlined in Table 7.3.

Previously, it was assumed that the core constructs of relationship education are universal and that programmes work equally well for couples from diverse backgrounds. However, from increasing work with disadvantaged communities and greater links with practitioners, more is now known about the challenges faced and the need to amend programme content to the specific needs of different communities.

Exploring the role of practitioners in conflict interventions

Most of the earlier evaluations of relationship-based interventions have been conducted in university settings with highly trained mental health professionals delivering the programme to modest numbers of volunteers. To have a wider reach and impact on relationship issues such as inter-parental conflict, promoting access to interventions and support is necessary. Widespread delivery could be achieved by embedding interventions in services already accessed and trusted by couples (Halford et al., 2008). There is some evidence that people other than mental health professionals, such as religious leaders (Markman et al., 2007) and midwives (Halford et al., 2008), can deliver couple relationship programmes effectively and with results similar to those achieved by mental health university staff.

Results, however, do seem to vary based on the target group as well as the type of intervention delivered. In a meta-analysis of couple-focused interventions with expectant and new parents, stronger effects were found if the interventions were led by professionals rather than semi-professionals. Well-trained practitioners such as family therapists may be more able to develop and implement adequate strategies for addressing these new parents' needs (Pinquart and Teubert, 2010). Further research suggests that highly trained professionals have the necessary skills and experience to successfully implement a less structured curriculum-based intervention, such as those which rely on group discussion (Wetzler et al., 2011). Volunteers or lay practitioners, however, may lack the broader expertise or mindset that comes with professional training to respond to individual needs (Rutter, 2010). This is less of an issue for highly structured curriculum-based interventions.

As with all intervention delivery, there is a need to balance efficacy (how the programme works in optimal conditions) and effectiveness (how it works in the real world). Although implementation in the community with practitioners of varied skills and experience is likely to produce more modest benefits, it does represent application in the 'real world', which should be a goal of intervention programmes (Rutter, 2010).

Home visitors and those in regular contact with parents, such as midwives, health visitors, family support workers etc., are in a position to provide information about how to buffer children from the effects of conflict and, if possible, how to develop better ways of managing conflict. They could also be used more widely to help promote and even deliver more structured curriculum-based interventions. More research in this area would be useful to explore what level of training and fidelity is necessary to sustain programme effectiveness and lead to positive outcomes for parents and children.

The review of existing couple interventions does suggest that although some improvements in couple interactions and conflict are shown, these are often focused on short-term changes and additional support may be needed to change behaviours on a more long-term basis. One potential way in which practitioners could assist behaviour change could be through using Motivational Interviewing techniques. This goes beyond simply providing knowledge and focuses on directly increasing the motivation to change target behaviour, in this case destructive forms of conflict. Motivational Interviewing has been used in a wide range of settings and a review of several meta-analyses indicate it is significantly more effective than no treatment (Lundahl and Burke, 2009). Recent evidence indicates that training level and the profession of the practitioner does not significantly influence Motivational Interviewing outcomes (Lundahl et al., 2009). However, empirical work in this area has mainly focused on alcohol and substance abuse; there is a need to assess the outcome of this approach in other areas and to determine whether it offers a useful approach to dealing with inter-parental conflict.

Using self-directed and online mediums

Relationship-based interventions are traditionally delivered mainly as face-to-face programmes. However, to reach more couples and to reduce costs in delivering programmes, alternative self-directed methods have been explored (Halford et al., 2004).

Some couples may prefer to access interventions through self-directed programmes because of the greater flexibility they offer. Learners have control of when, where and how they will access the material (Halford et al., 2004). Self-administered programmes also eliminate travel demands, which is more convenient for couples, and can make participation possible in otherwise inaccessible programmes

Table 7.3: Ways to encourage low-income and high-risk couples to engage in couple-based conflict interventions*

Outreach
Offer the programme at a convenient time and place, and in settings where individuals feel most comfortable.
Offer support for barriers to attending, such as help with child care.
Use former programme participants as recruiters, who can speak first-hand about the benefits.
Forge meaningful collaborative relationships with agencies and practitioners working with the target population.
Content and delivery of the programme
Amend content aimed at the particular challenges and circumstances low-income couples with children may face (e.g. housing).
Be realistic about programme goals, taking into account where couples may be already and other challenges they may face.
Provide (or signpost to) additional support for a range of additional stresses and issues which may cause conflict (e.g. help with housing, job and health related issues).
Use terms the target population will be familiar with and examples they can relate to.
Actively engage participants. Encourage opportunities for discussion, skill building and use more visual materials; rely less on written materials and structured lecture and workbook type approaches.
Provide follow-up. This is especially important if participants encounter unexpected challenges or stress which prevent implementing what they have learnt; this could be via community mentors, monthly support groups or later booster sessions.

* Adapted from findings reported by Halford and colleagues (2006) and Ooms and Wilson (2004). Mirrored through the Supporting Healthy Marriage study (Hsueh et al., 2012).

for those living in remote areas (Halford and Simons, 2005). Furthermore, self-directed programmes allow for privacy, which may be preferred over group-based, face-to-face approaches (Doss et al., 2009).

The evaluation evidence on self-directed relationship programmes is a growing area, but existing reports provide mixed findings. Whilst some studies indicate that self-assisted delivery is less effective than face-to-face training (Cummings et al., 2008) others suggest that self-administered programmes have been successfully applied to enhancing both couple relationships (Halford et al., 2004) and parenting (Webster-Stratton and Hammond, 1998). There is more recent evidence which indicates that a web-based self-directed version of relationship education is as effective as traditional face-to-face relationship education (Duncan et al., 2009).

It is important to note that many studies of self-directed programmes often do not directly compare findings to equivalent face-to-face programmes. Those which do compare approaches often use limited research designs where the method of delivery (face-to-face compared to self-assisted) is confused by other variables (such as length of intervention and content). As more is uncovered about why certain interventions work and factors which affect outcomes, improvements can be made to self-directed programmes.

Another way to strengthen the effects of self-directed programmes is to combine them with support from professionals or those in regular contact with parents, to help sustain engagement and ensure skill development (Duncan et al., 2009; Petch and Halford, 2008). Again, more research is needed to investigate what forms of professional support (e.g., telephone calls, e-mails, home visits, or a combination) might enhance programme effectiveness.

Conclusions

This chapter explores the implications for working with couples and parents to help reduce the impact of inter-parental conflict on children.

Although there are limitations to the research evidence available, there have also been some developments made in the past 10 years in the couple intervention field, which help to inform practical solutions for helping families deal with inter-parental conflict. This includes an increase in longitudinal studies that measure outcomes over longer periods of time, a growing range of outcome measures assessed (in a move to supplement parental self-report measures), and greater efforts to explore a community approach to intervention rather than relying on delivery from high level mental health professionals.

There have also been efforts by some researchers to investigate who the interventions work best for and possible reasons why. However, there are still significant gaps in our knowledge of intervention effectiveness and, particularly, what elements of different interventions are central to the outcomes reported (Wadsworth and Markman, 2012). This chapter outlines what we know and what we still need to know about inter-parental conflict interventions aimed at improving outcomes for children.

To summarise

- Early intervention is important before conflict problems become entrenched. Working with couples or even individuals at an earlier stage may lead to greater success in changing destructive conflict behaviour and promoting effective communication and conflict resolution.
- In addition to interventions targeted at parents it may also be useful to support children who are exposed to inter-parental conflict. Particularly where parents are separated or divorced, children may need help to explore their understanding of what their parents' conflict means for them and ways to cope with this.
- Conflict interventions can include both an awareness raising or informational element as well as a skills building component.
- A flexible approach to conflict intervention is needed so that programmes can be tailored to the different needs and requirements of specific groups.
- Some couples and individuals may find delivery of conflict interventions in a group context useful. They can share and learn from others as well as seeing that they are not alone.
- Others, however, may prefer the greater flexibility, anonymity and accessibility that self-directed on-line programmes can offer.
- Practitioners and those in regular contact with parents are in a prime position to identify conflict issues experienced by some families. They can help to raise awareness about inter-parental conflict and the effects on children as well as taking a more active role in signposting parents to conflict interventions, or even deliver more structured interventions themselves.

CHAPTER 8

CONCLUSIONS AND RECOMMENDATIONS

Although conflict is a normal and necessary part of family life, this review has shown that how parents argue with one another can affect the happiness and adjustment of their children. Conflict, whether parents are together or apart, is particularly detrimental to children when it is frequent, unresolved, intense, and about the child. Meanwhile, couples who continue to positively relate to one another even in the midst of heated conflicts, and who can find ways to resolve an argument, are less vulnerable to relationship breakdown and their children are less at risk of developing emotional or behavioural difficulties. There is also initial evidence that children can learn from observing more constructive conflict behaviours modelled by their parents, which can in turn help them in their own social relationships.

Research over the past decade has provided deeper insight into, not only the outcomes for children of exposure to destructive conflict, but also how children are affected and why some children appear more vulnerable than others. This knowledge is useful in terms of developing interventions to help couples and parents manage their conflict more effectively and avoid the potentially negative influence on their children. This chapter will briefly identify the headline findings from this review before addressing ways that practitioners, policy makers and researchers can help to support families experiencing conflict.

Headline findings

- Children exposed to conflict between parents are at risk of a range of negative outcomes including: emotional and behavioural difficulties (such as depression or aggression); trouble getting on with others; such as peers or family members; problems settling and achieving at school; sleep difficulties; and poorer physical health.
- Conflict between parents, not just the event of parental separation or divorce, is a key factor in explaining why some children fare worse than others when parental relationships breakdown.
- Conflict affects how couples parent and the quality of the relationship between parent and child. Parenting may be affected in a number of ways, with parents adopting a range of behaviours, from highly intrusive and hostile parenting through to lax, uninterested (or neglectful) parenting, all of which are associated with negative developmental outcomes for children.
- Emerging research also points to the influence of inter-parental conflict on specific neurobiological processes for the child, which in turn affects their emotional and cognitive functioning.
- Conflict within families has been found to pass from one generation to the next. This 'intergenerational transmission' of family conflict is not solely explained by genetic factors. Rather, family environmental factors such as inter-parental conflict and harsh parenting practices affect children's psychological development irrespective

of whether parents and children are genetically related or not.

- Some children are more vulnerable to the impact of conflict than others. Factors which may increase or decrease a child's vulnerability include: physiological make-up, temperament, age, support networks of peers, siblings or others, and coping strategies.
- Interventions to support couples experiencing or at risk of conflict can help improve aspects of the couple relationship, including patterns of interaction and communication. Important elements of such programmes include a specific focus on conflict and skills-based training.
- Intervening early, with young adults, newly-weds or those embarking on a long-term relationship, as well as couples going through the transition to parenthood, provides an opportunity to help couples before problems with conflict arise or become entrenched.
- Practitioners working with families, such as family support workers, health visitors or midwives, are well-placed to identify parents at risk of or struggling with conflict. With training, they may also provide information about conflict and relationship difficulties, sign-post families to more specialist support, or provide structured interventions themselves.

How practitioners can help families in conflict

The previous chapter highlighted how those who work closely with families are in a valuable position to help identify couples and parents who may be at risk of, or who already are experiencing, conflict in their relationship.

A midwife may pick up on signals from an expectant mother that she is worried about how the new baby will change things between her and her partner, noting that she has commented several times on areas where they disagree and have argued already. Meanwhile, a family support worker may notice during home visits that hostile exchanges between a child's mother and father are occurring in front of the child.

There are many professionals and other practitioners, such as those given in the examples above, who work with parents on a regular basis and who, over time, build a relationship of trust with families. Sometimes parents may turn to them directly for help with conflict related issues. Alternatively, the practitioner may suspect such problems exist by closely observing and picking up on both verbal and non-verbal clues that parents and perhaps children themselves give. Although some may feel experienced and confident enough to pick up on these areas with parents, it is likely that most would value specific training in ways to do this effectively. Many may also appreciate guidance on how they can help families to specifically deal with conflict and ways to improve outcomes for children.

Many of the couple intervention and prevention programmes reviewed in this book have been implemented by the programme developers themselves or researchers and highly trained academic professionals. More recently, there has been a move to explore ways of using innovative forms of delivering these programmes and using health practitioners and others who work regularly with families to help reach more families and to better target those most in need. Although further specific research on the outcome of practitioner led interventions are needed to better understand the most effective ways to achieve this, the conflict intervention literature reviewed here is useful in suggesting key ways in which practitioners can help families who are currently, or at risk of, experiencing conflict. These are discussed below and outlined in Box 8.1.

Gatekeepers to conflict interventions and further support

Training practitioners and family workers from various fields to recognise potential conflict difficulties in parents' relationships allows them to act as gatekeepers to conflict interventions. They are in a position to signpost parents to programmes and offer further support on conflict. In order to do this effectively, it is important that practitioners are aware of the local and national support and interventions available, and are able to understand and match these to the particular needs of the parents they are working with. Signposting is particularly important for complex cases that the practitioner is not trained to deal with, and where a specialist and targeted approach is needed, such as cases in which domestic violence or issues relating to drug or alcohol abuse are involved.

Promoting an early intervention approach and raising awareness

Practitioners on the front-line, working face-to-face with families, can offer an important avenue for promoting early conflict intervention. This can be achieved by identifying families or couples who may be at increased risk of experiencing later conflict and by picking up on signs of early relationship stress, before conflict problems arise. These practitioners can help to raise awareness for parents about what types of conflict can be harmful for children, the ways this conflict can impact on children's development, and how children may react differently to conflict.

This information needs to be delivered in a non-judgemental and parent-accessible way in order to highlight that not all conflict is bad and to motivate parents to want to change destructive types of conflict.

Help parents develop skills to avoid destructive conflict and to promote constructive conflict

Simply raising awareness about the impact of inter-parental conflict on children and how this occurs may not be enough to improve things for families or to avoid the negative impact on children. Practitioners may be in a position not only to inform parents about the potential impact of inter-parental conflict, but may also help parents to develop the skills needed to avoid using destructive conflict and to replace them with more effective ways of interacting with their child's father or mother.

They may take an active role in delivering more structured conflict interventions that aim to teach parents to use less negative conflict interactions such as physical or verbal aggression and withdrawing or walking away, whilst encouraging the development of problem solving and conflict resolution strategies. This could be provided in group sessions or through more one-to-one support with families.

Inform programme developers in how to customise conflict interventions

Practitioners' insights into families' lives and the wants, needs and challenges faced by particular groups of parents means that they can offer valuable information to intervention programme developers. In the previous chapter, it was suggested that a flexible approach to conflict intervention may be best in order to tailor programmes to the specific needs and requirements of different groups, especially groups of 'at risk' or hard to reach parents. Those who work closely with such parents can advise on how best to access these families, in addition to informing decisions on suitable content and delivery. They can help programme developers to understand the appropriate language to use, as well as what examples and specific issues are relevant.

Follow-up support for parents

Practitioners may also help facilitate conflict interventions by offering parents further support and following up on progress after they have completed a conflict intervention. Parents may need help in applying what they have learnt to everyday situations and in practising the new skills learnt, especially in challenging or stressful situations. A practitioner who has regular contact with parents and who has built up rapport and trust with them could encourage parents to reflect on what they learnt and any changes made since the programme. Where no changes have been made, or parents are struggling, they could be helped to think of ways to overcome barriers and challenges so that they can put into place what they learnt from the intervention programmes. This supportive approach from practitioners may be particularly useful for more self-assisted programmes and in encouraging more long-term behavioural change.

Box 8.1. Working with couples experiencing conflict

- The first step in helping families who are currently, or at risk of, experiencing conflict is to understand why parental conflict matters and how it can affect children.
- It is important to remember that it is not the conflict per se which matters but how parents argue.
- Identifying signs of direct and indirect destructive conflict and whether a family is experiencing problems (e.g. by how parents relate to one another or talk about one another, as well as their child's behaviour, etc.) is key.
- Relationship based training can help to increase practitioner confidence in how to talk to parents about conflict and problems in their relationship, without taking on a counselling role; and how to refer parents to further support if needed (Simons et al., 2003).
- Specialised training can be provided so practitioners can implement conflict interventions or prevention programmes themselves. For those less experienced, a structured approach may be favoured, utilising specific resources in a guided way. A more flexible approach may be more suitable for highly experienced professionals, who can target the intervention to the needs of a specific family or group.
- Training parents in skills related to constructive conflict and reducing destructive conflict styles of interactions may be beneficial. This training may need to be adapted based on parents, existing levels of interaction, as well as the presence of existing stressors and restrictions to engaging in such interventions.
- In addition to working on skills development, helping couples to build more positive ways of interacting and supporting one another may also be useful.

> • Times of stress and change may offer key opportunities to engage with couples and help improve interactions and ultimately outcomes for children and families.

The review of couple-based conflict programmes has been used by OnePlusOne to develop a blended learning (mix of online, face-to-face training and interactive resources for parents) training programme for practitioners. The 'How to Argue Better' programme is designed to help practitioners work with families experiencing conflict. Further research into the effectiveness of practitioner led interventions will help to develop this training further.

Focusing on children

This review has addressed how inter-parental conflict affects children in two key ways. First, children are affected because conflict affects how couples parent and the quality of relationship between parent and child. Secondly, how children understand, experience and respond to conflict between parents is also important.

Many of the interventions which link to inter-parental conflict have focused on the first pathway and explored ways of improving the couple relationship in order to improve parenting, and to prevent the spill-over effect onto the parent–child relationship. As identified earlier, there are few conflict interventions which are directed at, or which involve, children. Although it may be easier to work directly with parents, acknowledging that what children think about and how they experience conflict between their parents is important in understanding how they are likely to react. Where children have been exposed to prolonged destructive conflict, perhaps before and after parental separation, they may need additional help in ways to cope with their feelings associated with this conflict. Children need to feel secure in the love and care from their parents.

Encouraging help seeking

Although some parents may turn to others for help when they experience difficulties in their relationship, many may choose not to. Most couples view what happens in their relationship as private and not something that they want to share with others. Those who do turn to others for help may sometimes find that the advice they receive is ineffective or that well meaning friends and relatives can sometimes make the situation worse. To increase the reach of conflict interventions and to help families when they need it, it seems that more still needs to be done to make help-seeking easier. Help seeking could be encouraged by the following:

- *Normalising problems:* Raising awareness that most couples go through difficult times during their relationship could help to remove the stigma of looking for and accepting help during key relationship transitions.
- *Informing parents:* Even when parents decide they would like help, they may not know where to turn. Opening up avenues of signposting to relevant support could make a difference.
- *Being confident about what works:* Having evidence about what works and which conflict interventions can make a difference to families may encourage parents to take up various programmes which are available to them. A key part of increasing confidence about what works is ensuring that intervention programmes are robustly

evaluated and that the findings are disseminated to both parents and those who work with families, in a language and format that is accessible to them.

- *Increasing accessibility:* In addition to the above, another way to promote help seeking and encourage parents to take up preventative conflict interventions is to increase the accessibility of these programmes by exploring and evaluating new and innovative methods of delivery.

How policy makers can help

Policy makers can play an important role in helping families who may be at risk or who already are experiencing conflict, without being prescriptive or intruding into family affairs. Understanding the importance of couple relationships on outcomes for children and the family can help policy makers make informed decisions about funding and support for families.

Policy makers are in a position to promote awareness about inter-parental conflict and the impact on children. They can also help parents access information about what support is available to them so that they can make informed decisions about whether they want help and, if so, what help to take up.

Assessing the effectiveness of conflict interventions is a crucial part of the process in understanding what works for families and promoting the best outcomes for children. To do this successfully, both the short-term and long-term effects of programmes need to be explored and this takes both time and funding.

On a wider scale, family and economic policies can impact on the stresses that parents experience and this can influence the couple relationship, perhaps by making conflicts more intense and common. Where possible, supporting families through employment opportunities, improving working environments and childcare provision can help parents to cope better with normal everyday stresses and encourage raising happy children.

The role of further research

Over the past decade, there seems to have been considerable advances in research in the area of inter-parental conflict. As a consequence, we now know more about why and what aspects of inter-parental conflict matter, how it can impact on children and who is more vulnerable to negative outcomes, as well as what can be done about it. These areas are outlined in this current review.

Despite these advances, there is still much to learn in order to continue to improve outcomes for families. Key areas include: further evidence on whether constructive conflict can actually lead to positive developmental outcomes for children, exploring in more detail about how and why particular interventions work, and the mechanisms that mediate change. Another useful area for further research are longer-term studies which test the effectiveness of new and innovative intervention programme delivery. For example, assessing how practitioners can effectively help in programme delivery will help to understand how interventions can best be applied to real life settings. To assist the process of future research and to ensure that proven effective interventions are available to families, it is necessary for researchers, programme developers, practitioners and policy makers to work together.

REFERENCES

Ablow, J.C. & Measelle, J.R. (2009). Capturing young children's perceptions of marital conflict. In M. C. Schulz, M. Kline Pruett, P.K. Kerig, and R.D. Parke (Eds). *Strengthening Couple Relationships for optimal child development: lessons from research and intervention.* Washington, DC: American Psychological Association.

Almeida, D.M., Wethington, E. & Chandler, A. (1999). Daily spillover between marital and parent child conflict. *Journal of Marriage and the Family*, 61(1), 49-61.

Amato, P.R. (2005). The impact of family formation change on the cognitive, social and emotional wellbeing of the next generation. *Future of Children*, 15 (2), 75-96.

Amato, P.R. & Keith, B. (1991). Parental divorce and the wellbeing of children: A meta-analysis. *Psychological Bulletin*, 110(1), 26-46.

Appleyard, K., Egeland, B., van Dulmen, M.H. & Sroufe L.A. (2005). When more is not better: The role of cumulative risk in child behaviour outcomes. *Journal of Child Psychology and Psychiatry*, 46(3), 235-245.

Baldwin, T. T. (1992). The effects of alternative modeling strategies on outcomes of interpersonal-skills training. *Journal of Applied Psychology*, 77, 147–154.

Bandura, A. (1977). Self-efficacy: Toward a unifying theory of behavioral change. *Psychological Review*, 84, 191-215.

Bascoe S.M., Davies P.T., Sturge-Apple M.L. & Cummings E.M. (2009). Children's representations of family relationships, peer information processing, and school adjustment. *Developmental Psychoology*, 45(6), 1740-51.

Beaujouan, E. & Bhrolcháin, M. (2011). Cohabitation and marriage in Britain since the 1970s. Population Ttrends, 145.

Benson M., Buehler C. & Gerard J. (2008). Interparental Hostility and Early Adolescent Problem Behavior Spillover via Maternal Acceptance, Harshness, Inconsistency, and Intrusiveness. *Journal of Early Adolescence*, 28(3), 428-454

Birditt, K.S., Brown, E., Orbuch, T.L. & McIlvane, J.M. (2010). Marital Conflict Behaviors and Implications for Divorce Over 16 Years. *Journal of Marriage and Family*, 72(5), 1188–1204.

Blanchard, V.L., Hawkins, A.J., Baldwin, S.A. & Fawcett, E.B. (2009). Investigating the effects of marriage and relationship education on couples' communication skills: meta-analytic study. *Journal of Family Psychology*, 23(2), 203-214.

Blodgett Salafia, E.H., Gondoli, D.M. & Grundy, A.M. (2008). Marital conflict as a mediator of the longitudinal connections between maternal emotional distress and early adolescent maladjustment. *Journal of Child and Family Studies*, 17(6), 928-950.

Blum, R.W., Beuhring, T., Shew, M.L., Bearinger, L.H., Sieving, R.E. & Resnick. M.D. (2000). The effects of race/ethnicity, income, and family structure on adolescent risk behaviors. *American Journal of Public Health*, 90(12), 1879-1884.

Bradford, V. & Barber, B. (2008). When there is conflict: Interparental conflict, parent–child conflict, and youth problem behaviors. *Journal of Family Issues,* 29(6), 780-805.

Bradford, K., Barber, B., Olsen, J., Maughan, S., Erickson, L., Ward, D. && Stolz, H., (2004). A multi-national study of interparental conflict, parenting, and adolescent functioning. *Marriage and Family Review,* 35(3-4).

Bradbury T. & Karney B. (2004). Understanding and altering the course of intimate partnerships. *Social Policy Journal of New Zealand,* 23, 1-30

Bradbury, T.N. & Karney, B.R. (2004). Understanding and altering the longitudinal course of marriage. *Journal of Marriage and Family,* 66(4), 862-879.

Bradbury, T. N. & Lavner, J.A. (2012). How can we improve preventative and educational interventions for intimate relationships? *Behavior Therapy, 43,* 113-122.

Brooks-Gunn, J. & Duncan, G. J. (1997). The effects of poverty on children. *The Future of Children,* 7(2), 55-71.

Brown, L. D., Goslin, M. C. & Feinberg, M. E. (2011). Relating engagement to outcomes in prevention: The case of a parenting program for couples. *American Journal of Community Psychology,* doi:10.1007/s10464-011-9467-5.

Buchanan, C.M., Maccoby, E.E., & Dornbusch, S.M. (1991). Caught between parents: Adolescents' experience in divorced homes. *Child Development,* 62(5), 1008-1029.

Buehler, C,. Benson, M. & Gerard, J. (2006). Interparental hostility and early adolescent problem behavior: The mediating role of specific aspects of parenting. *Journal of Research on Adolescence,* 16(2), 265-292.

Buehler, C. & Gerard, J. (2002). Marital conflict, ineffective parenting, and children's and adolescents' maladjustment. *Journal of Marriage and Family,* 64(1), 78-92.

Buehler, C., Lange, G., & Franck, K. L. (2007). Adolescents' cognitive and emotional responses to marital hositility. *Child Development*, 78, 775-789.

Buehler, C. & Welsh, P. A. (2009). A process model of adolescents' triangulation into parents' marital conflict: The role of emotional reactivity. *Journal of Family Psychology*, 23(2), 167–180.

Capaldi, D. M., Pears, K. C., Patterson, G. R. & Owen, L. D. (2003). Continuity of parenting practices across generations in an at-risk sample: A prospective comparison of direct and mediated associations. *Journal of Abnormal Child Psychology*, 31(2), 127-142.

Carroll, J. S. & Doherty, W. J. (2003). Evaluating the effectiveness of premarital prevention programs: A meta-analytic review of outcome research. *Family Relations*, 52(2), 105-118.

Casey L. (2012) *Listen to troubled families*. London: Department for Communities and Local Government.

Coleman, L. (2011). Improving relationship satisfaction – Qualitative insights derived from individuals currently within a couple relationship. *The Family Journal*, 19(4), 369-380.

Coleman, L. & Glenn, F. (2009). *When couples part: Understanding the consequences for adults and children*. London: OnePlusOne.

Clements, M.L., Stanley, S.M. & Markman, H.J. (2004). Before they said 'I do': discriminating among marital outcomes over 13 years based on premarital data. *Journal of Marriage and Family*, 66(3), 613-626.

Conger, R.D., Conger, K.J., Elder, G.H. Jr, Lorenz, F.O., Simons, R.L. & Whitbeck, L.B. (1992). A family process model of economic hardship and adjustment of early adolescent boys. *Child Development*, 63(3), 526-541.

Conger, R.D., Ge, X., Elder, G.H., Jr., Lorenz, F.O. & Simons, R.L. (1994). Economic stress, coercive family process and developmental problems of adolescents. *Child Development,* 65(2), 541-561.

Conger, R.D., Conger, K.J., Matthews, L.S. & Elder, G.H., Jr. (1999). Pathways of economic influence on adolescent adjustment. *American Journal of Community Psychology,* 27(4), 519-541.

Cookston, J.T., Braver, S.L., Griffin, W.A., De Luse, S.R. & Miles, J.C. (2006). Effects of the Dads for Life interventions on interparental conflict and coparenting in the two years after divorce. *Family Process,* 46(1), 123-137.

Cookston, J.T. & Fung, W.W. (2011). The Kids' Turn program evaluation: Probing change within a community-based intervention for separating families. *Family Court Review,* 49(2), 348-363.

Cowan, C.P. & Cowan, P.A. (2000). *When Partners become Parents: The Big Life Change for Couples.* Mahwah, NJ: Erlbaum.

Cowan, P.A., Cowan, C.P., Ablow, J.C. Johnson, V. & Measelle, J.R. (2005). The family context of parenting in children's adaptation to school: Support for early intervention. In M.H. Bornstein (Series Editor), *Monographs in Parenting.* Manwah, NJ: Erlbaum Publishers.

Cowan, C.P., Cowan, P.A. & Barry, J. (2011). Couples' groups for parents of preschoolers: Ten-year outcomes of a randomized trial. *Journal of Family Psychology,* 25(2), 240-250.

Cowan, P.A., Cowan, C.P. & Knox, V. (2010). Marriage and fatherhood programs. *Future Child,* 20(2), 205-30.

Cowan, C.P., Cowan, P., Pruett, M.K. & Pruett, K. (2007). An approach to preventing coparenting conflict and divorce in low-income families: Strengthening couple relationships and fostering fathers' involvement. *Family Processes*, 46(1), 109-121.

Cowan, P.A., Cowan, C.P., Pruett, M.K., Pruett, K. & Wong, J.J. (2009). Promoting fathers' engagement with children: Preventative interventions for low-income families. *Journal of Marriage and Family*, 71(3), 663-679.

Cox, M., Paley, B. & Payne, C.C. (1997). *Marital and parent–child relationships*. Paper presented at the Biennial Meeting of the Society for Research in Child Development (Washington, DC).

Cox, M., Paley, B. & Harter, K. (2001). Interparental conflict and parent–child relationships. In, J.H. Grych and F.D. Fincham (Eds), *Interparental Conflict and Child Development: Theory, Research and Application*. New York: Cambridge University Press.

Criss, M. M., Pettit, G.S., Bates, J., Dodge, K.A. & Lapp, A. (2002). Family adversity, positive peer relationships, and children's externalizing behavior: A longitudinal perspective on risk and resilience. *Child Development*, 73(4), 1220-1237.

Crockenberg, S. & Langrock, A. (2001). The role of emotion and emotional regulation in children's responses to interparental conflict. In, J.H. Grych and F.D. Fincham (Eds), *Interparental Conflict and Child Development: Theory, Research and Application*, 129-16. New York: Cambridge University Press.

Crockenberg, S., Leerkes, E. & Lekka, S. (2007). Pathways from marital aggression to infant emotion regulation: The development of withdrawal in infancy. *Infant Behaviour and Development*, 30(1), 97-113.

Cui, M. & Fincham, F. (2010). The differential effects of parental divorce and marital conflict on young adult romantic relationships. *Personal Relationships*, 17(3), 331-343

Cummings, E.M., Ballard, M. & El-Sheikh, M. (1991). Responses of children and adolescents to interadult anger as a function of gender, age, and mode of expression. *Merrill-Palmer Quarterly*, 37(4), 543-560.

Cummings, E.M. & Davies, P.T. (1994). *Children and Marital Conflict: The Impact of Family Dispute and Resolution*. New York: Guilford Press.

Cummings, E.M. & Davies, PT. (1996) Emotional security as a regulatory process in normal development and the development of psycopathology. *Development and Psychopathology*, 8(1), 123-139.

Cummings, E.M. & Davies, P.T. (2002). Effects of marital conflict on children: Recent advances and emerging themes in process-oriented research. *Journal of Child Psychology and Psychiatry*, 43(1), 31-63.

Cummings E.M. & Davies, P.T. (2010) *Marital Conflict and Children: An Emotional Security Perspective*. New York: The Guilford Press.

Cummings, E.M., Davies, P.T. & Campbell, S.B. (2000). *Developmental psychopathology and family process. Theory, research and clinical implications*. New York: The Guilford Press.

Cummings, E.M., El-Sheikh, M., Kouros, C.D. & Keller, P.S. (2007). Children's skin conductance reactivity as a mechanism of risk in the context of parental depressive symptoms. *Journal of Child Psychology and Psychiatry*, 48(5), 436-445.

Cummings, E.M., Faircloth, W.B., Mitchell, P.M., Cummings, J. & Schermerhorn, A.C. (2008). Evaluating a brief prevention program for improving marital conflict in community families. *Journal of Family Psychology*, 22(2), 193-202.

Cummings, E.M., Goeke-Morey, M.C. & Papp, L.M. (2003). Children's responses to everyday marital conflict tactics in the home. *Child Development*, 74(6), 1918-1929.

Cummings, E.M., Goeke-Morey, M.C. & Papp, L.M. (2004). Everyday marital conflicts and child aggression. *Journal of Abnormal Child Psychology*, 32(2), 191-202.

Cummings, E.M., Goeke-Morey, M.C., Papp, L.M. & Dukewich, T.L. (2002). Children's responses to mothers' and fathers' emotionality and conflict tactics during marital conflict in the home. *Journal of Family Psychology*, 16(4), 478-492.

Cummings, E.M., Keller, P. & Davies, P. (2005). Towards a family process model of maternal and paternal depressive symptoms: Exploring multiple relations with child and family functioning. *Journal of Child Psychology and Psychiatry*, 46(5), 479-489.

Cummings, E.M., Lannotti, R.J. & Zahn-Waxler, C. (1989) Aggression between peers in early childhood. Individual continuity and developmental change. *Child Development*, 60(4), 887-895.

Cummings, E.M. & Merrilees, C.E. (2009). Identifying the dynamic processes underlying links between marital conflict and child adjustment. In, M. C. Schulz, M. Kline Pruett, P.K. Kerig, and R.D. Parke (Eds). *Strengthening Couple Relationships for Optimal Child Development: Lessons from Research and Intervention*, 27-40. Washington DC: American Psychological Association.

Cummings, E.M. & O'Reilly, A.W. (1997). Fathers in family context: Effects of marital quality on child adjustment. In M.E. Lamb (Ed), *The Role of the Father in Child Development,* 49-65. New York: Wiley.

Cummings, E.M., Schermerhorn, A.C., Davies, P.T, Goeke-Morey, M.C., & Cummings, J.S., (2006). Interparental discord and child adjustment: Prospective investigations of emotional security as an explanatory mechanism. *Child Development,* 77(1), 132-152

Cummings, E.M., Vogel, D., Cummings, J.S. & El-Sheikh, M. (1989) Children's responses to different forms of expression of anger between adults. *Child Development,* 60(6), 1392-1404.

Cummings, E.M. & Wilson, A.G. (1999). Contexts of marital conflict and children's emotional security: Exploring the distinction between constructive and destructive conflict from the children's perspective. In M. Cox and J. Brookes-Gunn (Eds), *Formation, Functioning and Stability of Families,* 105-129. Mahwah, NJ: Lawrence Erlbaum.

Cummings, E.M., Wilson, J. & Shamir, H. (2003). Reactions of Chilean and American children to marital discord. *International Journal of Behavioural Development,* 27(5), 437-444.

David, K. & Murphy, B. (2004). Interparental conflict and late adolescents' sensitisation to conflict: The moderating effects of emotional functioning and gender. *Journal of Youth and Adolescence,* 33(3), 187-200.

David, K. & Murphy, B. (2007). Interparental conflict and preschoolers' peer relations: The moderating roles of temperament and gender. *Social Development,* 16(1), 1-23.

Davies, P.T. & Cummings, E.M. (1994). Marital conflict and child adjustment: an emotional security hypothesis. *Psychological Bulletin,* 116(3), 387–411.

Davies, P.T. & Cummings, E.M. (2006) Interparental discord, family process and developmental psychopathology. In D. Cicchetti & D. J. Cohen (Eds.), *Developmental Psychopathology: Vol. 3: Risk, Disorder, and Adaptation (2nd ed.)*, 86-128. New York: Wiley & Sons.

Davies, P.T., Cummings, E.M. & Winter, M. A., (2004) Pathways between profiles of family functioning, child security in the interparental subsystem, and child psychological problems. *Development and Psychopathology*, 16(3), 525–550.

Davies, P.T., Harold, G., Goeke-Morey M.C., Marcie, C. & Cummings, E.M. (2002). Child emotional security and interparental conflict. *Monographs of the Society for Research in Child Development*, 67(3), 1-115.

Davies, P.T. & Lindsay, L.L. (2001). Does gender moderate the effects of marital conflict on children? In, J.H. Grych and F.D. Fincham (Eds). *Interparental Conflict and Child Development: Theory, Research and Application*. New York: Cambridge University Press.

Davies, P.T., Myers, R. L. & Cummings, E.M. (1996). Responses of children and adolescents to marital conflict scenarios as a function of the emotionality of conflict endings. *Merrill-Palmer Quarterly*, 42(1), 1-21.

Davies, P.T., Myers, R.L., Cummings, E.M. & Heindel, S. (1999). Adult conflict history and children's subsequent responses to conflict: An experimental test. *Journal of Family Psychology*, 13(4), 610-628.

Davies, P.T., Sturge-Apple, M.L., Cicchetti, D. & Cummings, E.M. (2007). The role of adrenocortical functioning in pathways between interparental conflict and child maladjustment. *Developmental Psychology*, 43(4), 918-930.

Davies, T., Sturge-Apple, M.L., Cicchetti, D. & Cummings, E.M. (2008). Adrenocortical underpinnings of children's psychological reactivity interparental conflict. *Child Development*, 79(6), 1693-1706.

Davies, P.T. Sturge-Apple M., Cicchetti D., Manning, L., Zale, E. (2009). Children's Patterns of Emotional Reactivity to Conflict as Explanatory Mechanisms in Links Between Interpartner Aggression and Child Physiological Functioning. *Journal of Child Psychology and Psychiatry*, 50(11), 1384-1391.

Davies, P.T., Sturge-Apple, M.L., Winter, M.A., Cummings, E.M. & Farrell, D. (2006). Child adaptational development in contexts of interparental conflict over time. *Child Development*, 77(1), 218–233.

Davies, P.T. & Windle, M. (2001). Interparental discord and adolescent adjustment trajectories: The potentiating and protective role of intrapersonal attributes. *Child Development*, 72(4), 1163-1178.

Davies, P.T., Woitach, M.J., Winter, M.A. & Cummings, E.M. (2008). Children's insecure representations of the interparental relationship and their school adjustment: The mediating role of attention difficulties. *Child Development*, 79(5), 1570-1582.

DeBoard-Lucas, R., Fosco, G., Raynor, S. & Grych, J. (2010). Interparental Conflict in Context: Exploring Relations Between Parenting Processes and Children's Conflict Appraisals. *Journal of Clinical Child and Adolescent Psychology*, 39(2), 163-175.

Dolan, P., Hallsworth, M., Halpern, D., King, D. & Vlaev, I. (2010). *Mindspace: Influencing behaviour through public policy*. London: Cabinet Office.

D'Onofrio, B.M., Turkheimer, E.N, Emery, R.E., Harden, K.P., Slutske, W., Heath, A., Madden, P.A.F & Martin, N.G. (2007). A genetically informed study of the intergenerational transmission of marital instability. *Journal of Marriage and Family,* 69(3), 793-803.

Doss, B.D., Rhoades, G.K., Stanley, S.M. & Markman, H.J. (2009). The effect of the transition to parenthood on relationship quality: An 8-year prospective study. *Journal of Personality and Social Psychology,* 96(3), 601–619.

Downey, G. & Coyne, J.C. (1990). Children of depressed parents: An integrative review. *Psychological Bulletin,* 108(1), 50-76.

Doyle, A.B. & Markiewicz, D. (2005). Parenting, marital conflict and adjustment from early- to mid-adolescence: Mediated by adolescent attachment style? *Journal of Youth and Adolescence,* 34(2), 97-110.

Driver, J., Tabares, A., Shapiro A., Young Nahm, E. & Gottman, J. (2003) Interaction patterns in marital success and failure: Gottman Laboratory Studies. In F. Walsh (Ed.) *Normal Family Processes. (3rd Edition). Growing Diversity and Complexity,* 493-513. New York: The Guilford Press.

Du Rocher Schudlich, T.D. & Cummings, E.M. (2003). Parental dysphoria and children's internalizing symptoms: Marital conflict styles as mediators of risk. *Child Development,* 74(6), 1663-1681.

Du Rocher Schudlich, T.D. & Cummings , E.M. (2007). Parental dysphoria and children's adjustment: marital conflict styles, children's emotional security, and parenting as mediators of risk. *Journal of Abnormal Child Psychology,* 35(4), 627-639

Du Rocher Schudlich, T.D., Papp, L. & Cummings, E.M. (2004). Relations of husbands' and wives' dysphoria to marital conflict resolution strategies. *Journal of Family Psychology*, 18(1), 171-183.

Du Rocher Schudlich, T.D., Shamir, H. & Cummings, E. M. (2004). Marital conflict, children's representations of family relationships, and children's dispositions towards peer conflict strategies. *Social Development,* 13(2), 171-191.

Duncan, S.F., Steed, A. & Needham, C.M. (2009). A comparison evaluation study of web-based and traditional marriage and relationship education. *Journal of Couple & Relationship Therapy,* 8(2), 162-180.

Dunn, J. (2002). Sibling Relationships. In P. Smith and C.H. Hart (Eds.), *Childhood Social Development*, 223-237. Oxford: Blackwell Publishers.

Dunn, J. & Davies, L. (2001). Sibling relationships and interparental conflict. In J.H. Grych and F.D. Fincham (Eds), *Interparental Conflict and Child Development: Theory, Research and Applications*, 273-290. New York: Cambridge University Press.

Dunn, J. & Deater-Deckard, K. (2001). *Children's views of their changing families.* Joseph Rowntree Foundation. York: York Publishing Services.

El-Sheikh, M. (2005) The role of emotional responses and physiological reactivity in the marital conflict-child functioning link. *Journal of Child Psychology and Psychiatry*, 46(11), 1191-1199.

El-Sheikh, M., Buckhalt, J.A., Cummings E.M. & Keller, P. (2007). Sleep disruptions and emotional insecurity are pathways of risk for children. *Journal of Child Psychology and Psychiatry,* 48(1), 88-96.

El-Sheikh, M., Buckhalt, J.A., Keller, P., Cummings, E.M. & Acebo, C. (2007a). Child emotional insecurity and academic achievement: the role of sleep disruptions. *Journal of Family Psychology*, 21(1), 29-38.

El-Sheikh, M., Buckhalt, J.A., Mize, J. & Acebo, C. (2006). Marital conflict and disruption of children's sleep. *Child Development*, 77(1), 31-43.

El-Sheikh, M. & Cummings, E.M., (1995). Children's responses to angry adult behaviours as a function of experimentally manipulated exposure to resolved and unresolved conflict. *Social Development*, 4(1), 75-91.

El-Sheikh, M., Cummings, E.M., Kouros, C.D., Elmore-Staton, L. & Buckhalt, J. (2008). Marital psychological and physical aggression and children's mental and physical health: direct, mediated, and moderated effects. *Journal of Consulting and Clinical Psychology*, 76(1), 138–148.

El-Sheikh, M., Cummings, E.M. & Reiter, S. (1996). Preschoolers' responses to interadult conflict: The role of experimentally manipulated exposure to resolved and unresolved arguments. *Journal of Abnormal Child Psychology*, 24(5), 665-679.

El-Sheikh, M. & Elmore-Staton, L. (2004). The link between marital conflict and child adjustment: Parent–child conflict and perceived attachments as mediators, potentiators, and mitigators of risk. *Development and Psychopathology*, 16(3), 631-648.

El-Sheikh, M. & Erath, S.A. (2011). Family conflict, autonomic nervous system functioning, and child adaptation: State of the science and future directions. *Development and Psychopathology*, 23(2), 703-721.

El-Sheikh, M., Harger, J. & Whitson, S.M. (2001). Exposure to interparental conflict and children's adjustment and physical health: The moderating role of vagal tone. *Child Development*, 72(6), 1617-1636.

El-Sheikh, M., Keller, P.S. & Erath, S.A. (2007). Marital conflict and risk for child maladjustment over time: skin conductance level reactivity as a vulnerability factor. *Journal of Abnormal Child Psychology*, 35(5), 715-727.

El-Sheikh, M., Kouros, C.D., Erath S., Cummings E.M., Keller, P. & Staton, L. (2009). Marital conflict and children's externalizing behavior: pathways involving interactions between parasympathetic and sympathetic nervous system activity. *Monograph of Society for Research into Child Development*, 74(1), vii–79.

El-Sheikh, M. & Reiter, S. (1996). Children's responding to live interadult conflict: the role of form of anger expression. *Journal of Abnormal Child Psychology*, 24(4), 401-415.

El-Sheikh, M. & Whitson, S. A. (2006). Longitudinal relations between marital conflict and child adjustment: Vagal regulation as a protective factor. *Journal of Family Psychology*, 20, 30-39.

Emery, R. E. (1982). Interparental conflict and the children of discord and divorce. *Psychological Bulletin*, 92, 310-330.

Erath, S.A. & Bierman, K.L. (2006). Aggressive marital conflict, maternal harsh punishment, and child aggressive-disruptive behavior: Evidence for direct and mediated relations. *Journal of Family Psychology*, 20(2), 217–226.

Erel, O. & Burman, B. (1995). Interrelatedness of marital relations and parent–child relations: A meta-analytic review. Psychological Bulletin, 118(1), 108-132.

Faircloth, W.B. & Cummings, E.M. (2008). Evaluating a parent education program for preventing the negative effects of marital conflict. *Journal of Applied Developmental Psychology*, 29(2), 141–156.

Faircloth, W.B., Schermerhorn, A.C., Mitchell, P.M., Cummings, J.S. & Cummings, E.M. (2011). Testing the long-term efficacy of a prevention program for improving marital conflict in community families. *Journal of Applied Developmental Psychology*, 32(4), 189-197.

Faks-Stewart, W., Kelley, M.L., Fincham, F.D., Golden, J., & Logsdon, T. (2004). Emotional and behavioral problems of children living with drug-abusing fathers: Comparisons with children living with alcohol-abusing and non-substance-abusing fathers. *Journal of Family Psychology*, 18(2), 319-330.

Fauber, R., Forehand, R., Thomas, A.M. & Wierson, M. (1990) A mediational model of the impact of marital conflict on adolescent adjustment in intact and divorced families: The role of disrupted parenting. *Child Development*, 61(4), 1112-1123.

Fawcett, E.B., Hawkins, A.J., Blanchard, V.L. & Carroll, J.S. (2010). Do premarital education programs really work? A meta-analytic study. *Family Relations*, 59(3), 232-239.

Feinberg, M.E., Jones, D.E., Kan, M.L. & Goslin, M.C. (2010). Effects of Family Foundations on parents and children: 3.5 years after baseline. *Journal of Family Psychology*, 24(5), 532-542.

Feinberg, M.E. & Kan, M.L. (2008). Establishing Family Foundations: Intervention effects on coparenting, parent/infant wellbeing, and parent–child relations. *Journal of Family Psychology*, 22(2), 253-263.

Feldman, R., Masalha, S. & Derdikman-Eiron, R. (2010). Conflict resolution in the parent–child, marital, and peer contexts and children's aggression in the peer group: A process-oriented cultural perspective. *Developmental Psychology*, 46(2), 310-25.

Fincham, F. & Beach, S. (1999). Conflict in marriage: Implications for working with couples. *Annual Review of Psychology*, 50, 47-77.

Finger, B., Eiden, R.D., Edwards, E.P., Leonard, K.E. & Kachadourian, L. (2010). Marital aggression and child peer competence: A comparison of three conceptual models. *Personal Relationships*, 17(3), 357-376.

Fosco, G.M. & Grych, J.H. (2007). Emotional expression in the family as a context for children's appraisals of interparental conflict. *Journal of Family Psychology*, 21, 248-258.

Fosco, G. & Grych, J. (2008). Emotional, cognitive, and family systems mediators of children's adjustment to interparental conflict. *Journal of Family Psychology*, 22(6), 843–854.

Franck, K.L. & Buehler, C. (2007). A family process model of marital hostility, parental depressive affect, and early adolescent problem behavior: The roles of triangulation and parental warmth. *Journal of Family Psychology*, 21(4), 614–625.

Frosch, C.A. & Mangelsdorf, S.C. (2001). Marital behavior, parenting behavior, and multiple reports of preschoolers' behavior problems: Mediation or moderation. *Developmental Psychology*, 37(4), 502–519.

Gardner, S.P. (2001). Evaluation of the 'Connection: Relationships and Marriage' curriculum. *Journal of Family and Consumer Sciences Education,* 19(1), 1-4.

Garriga, A. & Kiernan, K. (2013) Parents' relationship quality, mother–child relations and children's behaviour problems: evidence from the UK Millennium Cohort Study. Working Paper.http://www.york.ac.uk/media/spsw/documents/research-and-publications/Garriga-and-Kiernan-WP2013.pdf

Gelatt, V. A., Alder-Baeedr, F. & Seeley, J. R. (2010). An Interactive Web-Based Program For Stepfamilies: Development And Evaluation Efficacy. *Family Relations*, 59, 572-586.

Gerard, J., Buehler, C., Franck, K. & Anderson, O. (2005). In the eyes of the beholder: cognitive appraisals as mediators of the association between interparental conflict and youth maladjustment. *Journal of Family Psychology*, 19(3), 376–384.

Glade, A.C., Bean, R.A. & Vira, R. (2005). A prime time for marital/relational intervention: A review of the transition to parenthood literature with treatment recommendations. *The American Journal of Family Therapy*, 33(4), 319-336.

Glendinning, A., Shucksmith, J. & Hendry, L. (1997). Family life and smoking in adolescence. *Social Science and Medicine*, 44(1), 93-101.

Goeke-Morey, M.C., Cummings, E.M., Harold, G. T. & Shelton, K. H. (2002). Child responses to interparental conflict: Comparing the relative roles of emotional security and social learning processes. In P.T. Davies, G. T. Harold, M. C. Goeke-Morey & E. M. Cummings (Eds.,). Child Emotional Security and Interparental Conflict. *Monographs of the Society for Research on Child Development, Serial 270*, 67(3).

Goeke-Morey, M., Cummings, E.M., Harold, G.T. & Shelton, K.H. (2003). Categories and continua of destructive and constructive marital conflict tactics from the perspective of US and Welsh children. *Journal of Family Psychology*, 17(3), 327–338.

Goeke-Morey, M., Cummings, E.M. & Papp, L.M. (2007). Children and marital conflict resolution: Implications for emotional security and adjustment. *Journal of Family Psychology*, 21(4), 744-753.

Gonzales, N.A., Pitts, S.C., Hill, N.E. & Roosa, M.W. (2000). A mediational model of the impact of interparental conflict on child adjustment in a multiethnic, low-income sample. *Journal of Family Psychology*, 14(3), 365-379.

Goodman, M., Bonds, D., Sandler, I. & Braver, S. (2004). Parent psychoeducational programs and reducing the negative effects of interparental conflict following divorce. *Family Court Review*, 42(2), 263-279.

Goodman, A. & E. Greaves (2010). *Cohabitation, marriage and relationship stability*. Institute for Fiscal Studies: London.

Gordis, E.B., Margolin, G. & John, R. S. (1997). Marital aggression, observed parental hostility and child behaviour during triadic family interaction. *Journal of Family Psychology*, 11(1), 76-89.

Gordis, E. B., Margolin, G. & John, R. S. (2001). Parents' hostility in dyadic marital and triadic family settings and children's behavior problems. *Journal of Consulting and Clinical Psychology*, 69, 727-734.

Gore, S. Aseltine, R,.H. & Colten, M.E. (1993). Gender, social-relational involvement and depression. *Journal of Research on Adolescence*, 3(2), 101-125.

Gottman, J.M. (1994). *What predicts divorce?: The relationship between marital processes and marital outcomes*. Hillsdale, N.J: Lawrence Erlbaum Associates.

Gottman, J.M. & Katz, L.F. (1989). Effects of marital discord on your children's peer interaction and health. *Developmental Psychology,* 25(3), 373-381

Grass, K., Jenkins, J. & Dunn, J. (2007). Are sibling relationships protective? A longitudinal study. *Journal of Child Psychology and Psychiatry,* 48(2), 167–175.

Grych, J.H. (2005). Interparental conflict as a risk factor for child maladjustment: Implications for the development of prevention programs. *Family Court Review,* 43(10), 97-108.

Grych, J.H. & Cardoza-Fernandes, S. (2001). Understanding the impact of interparental conflict on children: The role of social cognitive processes In J.H. Grych and F.D. Fincham (Eds.), *Interparental Conflict and Child Development: Theory, Research and Application,* 157-187. New York: Cambridge University Press.

Grych, J.H. & Fincham F.D. (1990). Marital conflict and children's adjustment: A cognitive contextual framework. *Psychological Bulletin,* 108(2), 267-290.

Grych, J.H. & Fincham, F.D. (1993). Children's appraisals of marital conflict: Initial investigations of the cognitive-contextual framework. *Child Development,* 64(1), 215-230.

Grych, J.H. & Fincham, F.D. (2001). *Interparental conflict and child development: Theory, research and application.* New York: Cambridge University Press.

Grych, J. H., Fincham, F.D., Jouriles. E.N. & McDonald, R. (2000). Interparental conflict and child adjustment: Testing the meditational role of appraisals in the cognitive-contextual framework. *Child Development,* 71(6), 1648-1661.

Grych, J.H., Harold, G. & Miles, C. (2003). A prospective investigation of appraisals as mediators of the link between interparental conflict and child adjustment. *Child Development*, 74(4), 1176–1193.

Grych, J.H., Raynor, S.R. & Fosco, G.M. (2004). Family processes that shape the impact of interparental conflict on adolescents. *Development and Psychopathology*, 16(3), 649-65.

Halford, W.K. (2004). The future of couple relationship education: Suggestions on how it can make a difference. *Family Relations*, 53(5), 559-566.

Halford, W.K., Markman, H.J. & Stanley, S. (2008). Strengthening couples' relationships with education: Social policy and public health perspectives. *Journal of Family Psychology*, 22(3), 497-505.

Halford, W.K., Moore, E., Wilson, K.L., Farrugia, C. & Dyer, C. (2004). Benefits of flexible delivery relationship education: An evaluation of the Couple CARE program. *Family Relations,* 53(5), 469-475.

Halford, W.K., O'Donnell, C., Lizzio, A. & Wilson, K.L. (2006). Do couples at high risk of relationship problems attend premarriage education? *Journal of Family Psychology*, 20(1), 160-163.

Halford, W.K., Petch, J. & Creedy, D.K. (2010). Promoting a positive transition to parenthood: A randomized clinical trial of couple relationship education. *Prevention Science*, 11(1), 89-100.

Halford, W.K., Sanders, M.R. & Behrens, B.C. (2001). Can skills training prevent relationship problems in at-risk couples? Four-year effects of a behavioural relationship education program. *Journal of Family Psychology*, 15(4), 750-768.

Halford, W.K. & Simons, M. (2005). Couple relationship education in Australia. *Family Process*, 44(2), 147-159.

Halford, W. K., Wilson, K., Watson, B., Verner, T., Larson, J., Busby, D. & Holman, T. (2010). Couple relationship education at home: Does skill training enhance relationship assessment and feedback? *Journal of Family Psychology*, 24(2), 188-196.

Harold, G.T., Aitken, J.J. & Shelton, K.H. (2007). Inter-parental conflict and children's academic attainment: a longitudinal analysis. *Journal of Child Psychology and Psychiatry*, 48(12), 1223–1232.

Harold, G.T. & Conger, R.D. (1997). Marital conflict and adolescent distress: the role of adolescent awareness. *Child Development*, 68(2), 333-350.

Harold, G.T., Elam, K., Lewis, G., Rice, F., Thapar, A. (2013). Integrating family socialization and intergenerational transmission hypotheses underlying childhood antisocial behavior: the role of inter-parental conflict and passive-genotype environment correlation. *Development and Psychopathology*, 25(1), 37–50.

Harold, G.T. & Leve, L. (2012). Parents as partners: how the parental relationship affects children's psychological development. In A. Balfour, M. Morgan & C. Vincent (Eds.), *How Couple Relationships Shape Our World: Clinical Practice, Research and Policy Perspectives*. London: Tavistock Centre for Couple Relationships.

Harold, G.T. & Murch, M.A. (2005). Inter-parental conflict and children's adaptation to separation and divorce: Implications for family law, policy and practice. *Child and Family Law Quarterly*, 17(2), 185–206.

Harold, G.T., Pryor, J. & Reynolds, J. (2001). *Not in Front of the Children? How Conflict Between Parents Affects Children*. London: OnePlusOne.

Harold, G.T., Rice, F.J., Hay, D.F., Boivin, J., van den Bree, M. & Thapar, A. (2010). Familial transmission of depression and antisocial behaviour symptoms: Disentangling the contribution of inherited and environmental factors and testing the mediating role of parenting. *Psychological Medicine*, 41(6), 1175–1185.

Harold, G.T., Shelton, K., Goeke-Morey M.C. & Cummings, E.M. (2004). Child emotional security about family relationships and child adjustment. *Social Development*, 13(3), 350-376.

Hawkins, A.J., Blanchard, V.L., Baldwin, S.A. & Fawcett, E.B. (2008). Does marriage and relationship education work? A meta-analytic study. *Journal of Consulting and Clinical Psychology*, 76(5), 723-734.

Hawkins, A.J., Carroll, J. S., Doherty, W.J. & Willoughby, B. (2004). A comprehensive framework for marriage education. *Family Relations*, 53(5), 547-558.

Hawkins, A. J., Fawcett, E.B., Carroll, J. S. & Gilliland, T. T. (2006). The Marriage Moments program for couples transitioning to parenthood: divergent conclusions from formative and outcome evaluation data. *Journal of Family Psychology*, 20(4), 561-570.

Hetherington, E.M. & Stanley-Hagan, M. (1999). The adjustment of children with divorced parents: a risk and resiliency perspective. *Journal of Child Psychology and Psychiatry*, 40(1), 129-140.

Hipwell, A. E., Murray, L., Ducournau, P. & Stein, A. (2005) The effects of maternal depression and parental conflict on children's peer play The effects of maternal depression and parental conflict on children's peer play. *Child: Care, Health and Development*, 31 (1). pp. 11-23. ISSN 0305-1862

Holden, G. W., Geffner, R. & Jouriles, E. N. (1998). *Children exposed to marital violence: Theory, research, and applied issues.* Washington, DC: American Psychological Association.

Holden, G. & Ritchie, K. (1991). Linking extreme marital discord, child rearing and child behavior problems: evidence from battered women. *Child Development,* 62(2), 311-327.

Holt-Lunstad, J., Birmingham, W. & Jones, B. Q. (2008). Is there something unique about marriage? The relative impact of marital status, relationship quality, and network social support on ambulatory blood pressure and mental health. *Annals of Behavioural Medicine,* 35 (2), 239-244.

Hsueh, J. A., Alderson, D. P., Lundquist, E., Michalopoulos, C., Gubits, D., Fein, D. & Knox, V. (2012). *The supporting healthy marriage evaluation: early impacts on low-income families.* OPRE Report 2012-11. Washington, DC: Office of Planning, Research and Evaluation, administration for Children and Families, Department of Health and Human Services.

Hunt, S. A. (2009). *Family Trends: British families since the 1950s.* London: Family and Parenting Institute.

Huston T. L. & Holmes E. K. (2004). Becoming parents. In A. Vangelisti (Ed), *Handbook of Family Communication,* 105–133. Mahwah, NJ : Lawrence Erlbaum Associates.

Jenkins, J., Simpson, A., Dunn, J., Rasbash, J. & O'Connor, T. G. (2005). Mutual influence of marital conflict and children's behavior problems: Shared and nonshared family risks. *Child Development,* 76(1), 24–39.

Jenkins, J. M. & Smith, M. A. (1990). Factors protecting children living in disharmonious homes. *Journal of the American Academy of Child and Adolescent Psychiatry,* 29, 60-69.

Jenkins, J. & Smith, M.A. (1991). Marital disharmony and children's behavior problems: aspects of a poor marriage that affect children adversely. *Journal of Child Psychology and Psychiatry*, 32(5), 793-810.

Johnson, P.L. & O'Leary, K.D. (1987). Parental behaviour patterns and conduct disorders in girls. *Journal of Abnormal Child Psychology*, 15(4), 573-581.

Jouriles, E.N., Murphy, C. Farris, A.M., Smith, D.A., Richters, J.E. & Waters, E. (1991). Marital adjustment, childrearing disagreements, and child behaviour problems: Increasing the specificity of the marital assessment. *Child Development*, 62(6), 1424-1433.

Jouriles, E. N. & Norwood, W. D. (1995). Physical aggression toward boys and girls in families characterized by the battering of women. *Journal of Family Psychology*, 9, 69-78.

Jouriles, E.N., Spiller, L.C., Stephens, N., McDonald, R. & Swank, P. (2000). Variability in adjustment of children of battered women: The role of child appraisals of interparent conflict. *Cognitive Therapy and Research*, 24(2), 233-249.

Kari, H. & Kay, P. (2005). Conditions affecting the association between father identity and father involvement. *Fathering*, 3(1), 59-80.

Katz, F. (2001) Physiological processes as mediators of the impact of marital conflict. In J.H. Grych and F.D. Fincham (Eds), *Interparental Conflict and Child Development. Theory, Research and Application*, 188-212. New York: Cambridge University Press.

Katz, L.F. & Gottman, J.M. (1996). Spillover effects of marital conflict: in search of parenting and coparenting mechanisms. In J.P. McHale and P.A. Cowan (Eds), *New Directions for Child Development: Studies of Two-Parent Families*, 57-76. San Francisco: Jossey-Bass.

Katz, L.F. & Gottman, J.M. (1997). Buffering children from marital conflict and dissolution. *Journal of Clinical Child Psychology*, 26(2), 157-171.

Katz, L.F. & Windecker-Nelson, B. (2006). Domestic violence, emotion coaching, and child adjustment. *Journal of Family Psychology*, 20(1), 56-67.

Katz, L.F. & Woodin, E.M. (2002). Hostility, hostile detachment and conflict engagement in marriages: effects on child and family functioning. *Child Development*, 73(2), 636-651.

Keller, P. Cummings, E.M. & Davies, P. (2005). The role of marital discord and parenting in relations between parental problem drinking and child adjustment. *Journal of Child Psychology and Psychiatry*, 46(9), 943-951.

Keller, P.S., Cummings, E.M., Peterson, K.M., Davies, P.T. & Mitchel, P.M. (2008). Longitudinal relations between parental drinking problems, family functioning, and child adjustment. *Development and Psychopathology*, 20(1), 195-212.

Kelly, J.B. (2000). Children's adjustment in conflicted marriage and divorce: A decade review of research. *Journal of the American Academy of Child and Adolescent Psychiatry, 39*, 963-973.

Kelley, M. L., & Fals-Stewart, W (2002). Couples therapy for substance-abusing parents: Effects on children. *Journal of Consulting and Clinical Psychology, 20*, 417-427.

Kerig, P. (1996). Assessing the links between interparental conflict and child adjustment: the conflicts and problem-solving scales. *Journal of Family Psychology*, 10(4), 454-473.

Kerig, P. (2001). Children's coping with interparental conflict. In, J.H. Grych and F.D. Fincham (Eds), *Interparental Conflict and Child Development: Theory, Research and Application,* 213-248. New York: Cambridge University Press.

Kerig, P.K., Cowan. P.A. & Cowan, C.P. (1993). Marital quality and gender differences in parent–child interaction. *Developmental Psychology*, 29(6), 931-939.

Kerig, P. & Swanson, J.A., (2009). Ties that bind: triangulation, boundary dissolution, and the effects of interparental conflict on child development. In M. C. Schulz, M. Kline Pruett, P.K. Kerig, and R.D. Parke (Eds.), *Strengthening Couple Relationships for Optimal Child Development: Lessons from Research and Intervention.* Washington, DC: American Psychological Association.

Kinsfogel, K. & Grych, J.H. (2004). Interparental conflict and adolescent dating relationships: integrating cognitive, emotional, and peer influences. *Journal of Family Psychology*, 18(3), 505–515.

Kitzmann, K. (2000). Effects of marital conflict on subsequent triadic family interactions and parenting. *Developmental Psychology*, 36(1), 3-13.

Kitzmann, K.M., Gaylord, N.K., Holt, A,.R. & Kenny, E.D. (2003). Child witnesses to domestic violence: A meta-analytic review. *Journal of Consulting and Clinical Psychology*, 71(2), 339-352.

Knutson, L. & Olson, D. H. (2003). Effectiveness of PREPARE program with premarital couples in community settings. *Marriage & Family*, 6(4), 529-546.

Koss, K., George, M.R.W., Bergman, K N., Cummings, E.M., Davies, P.T. & Cicchetti, D. (2011). Understanding children's emotional processes and behavioral strategies in the context of marital conflict. *Journal of Experimental Child Psychology*, 109(3), 336-352.

Kramer, K. M., Arbuthnot, J., Gordon, D. A., Rousis, N. J., and Hoza, J. (1998): 'Effects of skill-based versus information-based divorce education programs on domestic violence and parental communication'. *Family and Conciliation Courts Review*, 36(1), 9-31.

Krishnakumar, A. & Buehler, C. (2000). Interparental conflict and parenting behaviours: A meta-analytic review. *Family Relations*, 49(1), 25-44.

Krishnakumar, A., Buehler, C. & Barber, B.K. (2003). Youth perceptions of interparental conflict, ineffective parenting, and youth problem behaviors in European-American and African-American families. *Journal of Social and Personal Relationships*, 20(2), 239–260.

Laumakis, M., Margolin, G. & John, R. (1998). The emotional, cognitive and coping responses of preadolescent children to different dimensions of marital conflict. In G,. Holden, B. Geffner, and E. Jouriles (Eds), *Children and Family Violence*, 257-288. Washington, DC: American Psychological Association:

Laurent, H. K., Leve, L. D., Neiderhiser, J. M., Natsuaki, M. N., Shaw, D. S., Fisher, P. A., Marceau, K., Harold, G. T. & Reiss, D. (in press). Effects of parental depressive symptoms on child adjustment moderated by HPA: Within- and between-family risk. *Child Development*.

Lavner, J.A. & Bradbury, T.N. (2012). Why do even satisfied newlyweds eventually go on to divorce? *Journal of Family Psychology*, 26(1), 1-10.

Leary, A. & Katz, L. F. (2004). Coparenting, family-level processes, and peer outcomes: The moderating role of vagal tone. *Development and Psychopathology*, 16, 593-608.

Lerner, J.V. (1983). The role of temperament in psychosocial adaptation in early adolescence: A test of a 'goodness of fit' model. *Journal of Genetic Psychology*, 143(2), 149-157.

Lindahl, K.M., Clements, M. & Markman, H. (1997). Predicting marital and parent functioning in dyads and triads: A longitudinal investigation of marital processes. *Journal of Family Psychology*, 11(2), 139-151.

Lindahl, K.M., Malik, N.M., Kaczynski, K. & Simons, J.S. (2004). Couple power dynamics, systemic family functioning, and child adjustment: A test of a mediational model in a multiethnic sample. *Development and Psychopathology*, 16(3), 609-630.

Lindsey, E.W., Colwell, M.J., Frabutt, J.M. & MacKinnon-Lewis, C. (2006). Family conflict in divorced and non-divorced families: Possible consequences for boys' mutual friendship and friendship quality. *Journal of Social and Personal Relationships*, 23(1), 45-63.

Lloyd, G. & Lacey, R. (2012). *Understanding 21ˢᵗ Century Relationships: A Compendium of Key Data*. London: OnePlusOne.

Lundahl, B. & Burke, B. L. (2009). The effectiveness and applicability of motivational interviewing: A practice-friendly review of four meta-analyses. *Journal of Clinical Psychology*, 65(11), 1232-1245.

Lundahl, B., Kunz, C., Brownell, C., Tollefson, D., & Burke, B. L. A meta-analysis of motivational interviewing: Twenty-five years of empirical studies. *Research on Social work Practice*, 20(2), 137-160.

Luster, T., & Okagaki, L. (2006). *Parenting: An ecological perspective. Second Edition.*Routledge.

Mannering, M., Harold, G.T., Level, L.D., Shelton, K.H., Shaw, D.D., Conger, R.D., Neiderhiser, J.M., Scaramella, L.V. & Reiss, D. (2011). Longitudinal associations between marital instability and child sleep problems across infancy and toddlerhood in adoptive families. *Child Development,* 82(4), 1252-1266.

Margolin, G., Christensen, A. & John, R.S. (1996). The continuance and spillover of everyday tensions in distressed and nondistressed families. *Journal of Family Psychology*, 10(3), 304-321.

Margolin, G., Gordis, E.B. & Oliver, P.H. (2004). Links between marital and parent–child interactions: Moderating role of husband-to-wife aggression. *Development and Psychopathology* 16(3), 753-771.

Margolin, G., Oliver, P.H. & Medina, A.M. (2001). Conceptual issues in understanding the relation between interparental conflict and child adjustment: Integrating developmental psychopathology and risk/resilience perspectives. In, J.H. Grych and F.D. Fincham (Eds), *Interparental Conflict and Child Development: Theory, Research and Application*. New York: Cambridge University Press.

Markman, H., Williams, T., Einhorn, L. & Stanley, S.M. (2007). The new frontier in relationship education: Innovations and challenges in dissemination. *Behavior Therapist*, 31(1), 14–17.

Marks, C.R., Glaser, B. A., Glass, J.B. & Horne, A.M., (2001). Effects of witnessing severe marital discord on children's social competence and behavioral problems. *The Family Journal*, 9(2), 94-101.

McCoy, K., Cummings, E. & Davies, P. (2009). Constructive and destructive marital conflict, emotional security, and children's prosocial behaviour. *Journal of Child Psychology and Psychiatry*, 50(3), 270-279.

McIntosh, J. & Deacon-Wood, H.B. (2003). Group interventions for separated parents in entrenched conflict: An exploration of evidence-based frameworks. *Journal of Family Studies*, 9(2), 187-199.

McLoyd, V.C. & Ceballo, R. (1998). Conceptualizing and assessing economic context: Issues in the study of race and child development. In V. C. McLoyd and L. Steinberg (Eds.), *Studying Minority Adolescents: Conceptual, Methodological, and Theoretical Issues*, 251-278. Mahwah, NJ: Erlbaum.

McMunn, A. M., Nazroo, J.Y., Marmot, M.G., Boreham, R. & Goodman, R. (2001). Children's emotional and behavioural wellbeing and the family environment: Findings from the Health Survey for England. *Social Science & Medicine*, 53(4), 423–440.

Minuchin, S., Rosman, B. & Baker, L. (1978). *Psychosomatic families: Anorexia nervosa in context*. Cambridge, MA: Harvard University Press.

Mitnick, D.M., Heyman, R.E. & Smith Slep, A.M. (2009). Changes in relationship satisfaction across the transition to parenthood: A meta-analysis. *Journal of Family Psychology*, 23(6), 848–852.

Modry-Mandell, K.L., Gamble W.C. & Taylor A.R. (2007) Family Emotional Climate and Sibling Relationship Quality: Influences on Behavioral Problems and Adaptation in Preschool-Aged Children. *Journal of Child and Family Studies*, 16(1), 59–71.

Montgomery, S.M., Bartley, M.J. & Wilkinson, R.G. (1997). Family conflict and slow growth. *Archives of Disease in Childhood*, 77(4), 326–30.

Mooney, A., Oliver, C. & Smith, M. (2009). *Impact of family breakdown on children's wellbeing: Evidence review*. London: Department of Children, Schools and Families (RB113).

Moore, G. (2010). Parent conflict predicts infants' vagal regulation in social interaction. *Development and Psychopatholgy*, 22(1), 23–33.

Morton, J.B., Trehub, S.E. & Zelazo, P. D. (2003). Sources of inflexibility in 6-year olds' understanding of emotion in speech. *Child Development*, 74(6), 1857–1868.

National Family and Parenting Institute (2000). *Teenagers' attitudes to parenting: A survey of young people's experiences of being parented and their views on how to bring up children*. (MORI survey) London: NFPI.

Nicolotti, L., El-Sheikh, M. & Whitson, S. M. (2003). Children's coping with marital conflict and their adjustment and physical health: Vulnerability and protective functions. *Journal of Family Psychology, 17,* 315-326.

Office for National Statistics. (2012). Divorces in England and Wales – 2011.

Office for National Statistics (2013a). Vital statistics: Population and health reference tables (February 2013 update): annual time series data.

Office for National Statistics (2013b). General Lifestyle Survey Overview – a report on the 2011 General Lifestyle Survey.

Olson, D.H. & Gorall, D.M. (2003). Circumplex model of marital and family systems. In F. Walsh (Ed.), *Normal Family Processes: Growing Diversity and Complexity (3rd Edition)*, 514-548. New York: Guilford.

Ooms, T. & Wilson, P. (2004). The challenges of offering relationship and marriage education to low-income populations. *Family Relations*, 53(5), 440-447.

OnePoll. (2009). *Rows*. Available from http://www. onepoll.com/op_press_view.php?width=800&height =600&id=563).

Osborne, L.N. & Fincham, F.D. (1996). Marital conflict, parent–child relationships, and child adjustment: Does gender matter? *Merrill-Palmer Quarterly*, 42(1), 48-75.

Parke, R., Kim, M., Flyr, M., McDowel, D.J., Simplinks, S., Killian, C. & Wild, M. (2001). Managing marital conflict: links with children's peer relationships. In J.H. Grych and F.D. Fincham (Eds), *Interparental Conflict and Child Development: Theory, Research and Application*. New York: Cambridge University Press.

Pauli-Pott, U. & Beckmann, D. (2007). On the association of interparental conflict with developing behavioral inhibition and behavior problems in early childhood. *Journal of Family Psychology*, 21(3), 529-532.

Pedro-Carroll, J.L. (1997). The children of divorce intervention program: Fostering resilient outcomes for school-aged children. In G.W. Albee & T. Gullotta (Eds.), *Primary Prevention Works*, 213-238. Thousand Oaks, CA: Sage.

Pedro-Carroll, J. (2005). Fostering children's resilience in the aftermath of divorce: The role of evidence-based programs for children. *Family Court Review*, 43(1), 52-64.

Petch, J. & Halford, W.K. (2008). Psycho-education to enhance couples' transition to parenthood. *Clinical Psychology Review*, 28(7), 1125-1137.

Pidd, K. (2004). The impact of workplace support and identity on training transfer: A case study of drug and alcohol safety training in Australia. *International Journal of Training and Development*, 8, 274-288.

Pinquart, M. & Tuebert, D. (2010). A meta-analytic study of couple interventions during the transition to parenthood. *Family Relations*, 59(3), 221-231.

Plomin, R. (1990). The role of inheritance in behavior. *Science*, 248(4952), 183–188.

Porges, S.W. (2007). The polyvagal perspective. *Biological Psychology*, 74(2), 116-143.

Pruett, M.K., Insabella, G.M. & Gustafson, K. (2005). The Collaborative Divorce Project: A court-based intervention for separating parents with young children. *Family Court Review*, 43(1), 38-51.

Pryor, J. & Rodgers, B. (2001). *Children in changing families: life after parental separation*. Oxford, UK: Blackwell Publishing.

Ramos, M.C., Guerin, D.W., Gottfried, A. W., Bathurst, K. & Oliver, P.H. (2005). Family conflict and children's behavior problems: The moderating role of child temperament. *Structural Equation Modelling*, 12(2), 278–298.

Repetti, R., Taylor, S. E. & Seeman, T.E. (2002). Risky families: family social environments and the mental and physical health of offspring. *Psychological Bulletin*, 128(2), 330–366.

Rhoades, K.A. (2008). Children's responses to interparental conflict: A meta-analysis of their associations with child adjustment. *Child Development*, 79(6), 1942-1956.

Rhoades, K.A., Leve, L.D., Harold, G.T., Neiderhiser, J.M., Shaw, D.S. & Reiss, D. (2011). Longitudinal pathways from marital hostility to child anger during toddlerhood: genetic susceptibility and indirect effects via harsh parenting. *Journal of Family Psychology*, 25(2), 282–291.

Rice, F., Harold, G.T., Shelton, K.H. & Thapar, A. (2006). Family conflict interacts with genetic liability in predicting childhood and adolescent depression. *Journal of the American Academy of Child and Adolescent Psychiatry*, 45(7), 841-8.

Richmond, M.K., & Stocker, C.M. (2003). Sibling's differential experiences of marital conflict and differences in psychological adjustment. *Journal of Family Psychology*, 17, 339-350.

Rivett, M., Howarth, E. & Harold, G. (2006). 'Watching from the stairs': towards an evidence-based practice in work with child witnesses of domestic violence. *Clinical Child Psychology and Psychiatry*, 11(1), 103–125.

Rogers, M.J. & Hombeck, G.N. (1997). Effects of interparental aggression on children's adjustment: The moderating role of cognitive appraisal and coping. *Journal of Family Psychology*, 11(1), 125-130.

Rohner, R.P. (2004). The parental 'acceptance-rejection syndrome': Universal correlates of perceived rejection. *American Psychologist*, 59(8), 830-840.

Rutter, M. (2006). *Genes and Behavior: Nature and Nurture Interplay Explained*. Oxford: Blackwell.

Rutter, M. (2010). *Social Science and Family Policies*. The British Academy.

Schacht, P.M., Cummings, E.M. & Davies, P. (2009). Fathering in family context and child adjustment: a longitudinal analysis. *Journal of Family Psychology*, 23(6), 790–797.

Schermerhorn, A., Cummings, E.M. & Davies, P. (2008). Children's representations of multiple family relationships: Organizational structure and development in early childhood. *Journal of Family Psychology*, 22(1), 89-101.

Schermerhorn, A., Cummings, E.M., DeCarlo, C. & Davies, P. (2007). Children's influence in the marital relationship. *Journal of Family Psychology*, 21(2), 259–269.

Schoppe-Sullivan, S.J., Schermerhorn, A. & Cummings, E.M. (2007). Marital conflict and children's adjustment: Evaluation of the parenting process model. *Journal of Marriage and Family*, 69(5), 1118-1134.

Schulz, M.S., Cowan, C.P. & Cowan, P.A. (2006). Promoting healthy beginnings: A randomized controlled trial of a preventative intervention to preserve marital quality during the transition to parenthood. *Journal of Consulting and Clinical Psychology*, 74(1), 20-31.

Shamir, H., Cummings, E. M., Davies, P. & Goeke-Morey, M. (2005). Children's Reactions to Marital Conflict in Israel and in the United States. *Parenting, Science and Practice*, 5(4), 371-386.

Shapiro, A. F. & Gottman, J. M. (2005). Effects on marriage of a psycho-communicative-educational intervention with couples undergoing the transition to parenthood, evaluation at 1-year post intervention. *The Journal of Family Communication*, 5(1), 1-24.

Shelton, K. & Harold, G.T. (2007). Marital conflict and children's adjustment: the mediating and moderating role of children's coping strategies. *Social Development*, 16(3), 497-512.

Shelton, K. & Harold, G.T. (2008). Cognitive appraisals and coping strategies psychological adjustment: Bridging links through children's pathways between interparental conflict and adolescent psychological adjustment. *Journal of Early Adolescence*, 28(4), 555-582.

Shifflett, K. & Cummings, E.M. (1999). A program for educating parents about the effects of divorce and conflict on children: An initial evaluation. *Family Relations*, 48(1), 79-89.

Siffert, A. & Schwarz, B. (2011). Parental conflict resolution styles and children's adjustment: Children's appraisals and emotion regulators as mediators. *Journal of Genetic Psychology*, 172(1), 21-39.

Sigal, A., Sandler., Wolchik, S. & Braver, S. (2011). Do parent education programs promote healthy postdivorce parenting? Critical distinctions and a review of the evidence. *Family Court Review*, 49(1), 120-139.

Simons, J., Reynolds, J., Mannion, J., Morison, L. (2003). How the health visitor can help when problems between parents add to postnatal stress. *Journal of Advanced Nursing* 44, 400–411.

Smart, C. Wade, A. & Neale, B. (2000). *New Childhoods: Children and Co-parenting after Divorce*. Children 5-16 Research Programme Briefing Paper 4. Swindon: ESRC.

Smart, C., Neale B. & Wade, A. (2001). *The Changing Experience of Childhood: Families and Divorce.* Cambridge: Polity Press.

Stanley, S.M., Amato, P.R., Johnson, C.A. & Markman, H.J. (2006). Premarital education, marital quality, and marital stability: Findings from a large, random household survey. *Journal of Family Psychology*, 20(1), 117-126.

Steinberg, L. & Avenevoli, S. (2000). The role of context in the development of psychopathoogy: A conceptual framework and some speculative propositions. *Child Development*, 71(1), 66-74.

Sternberg, K.J., Lamb, M.E., Greenbaum, C., Cicchetti, D., Dawud, S., Cortes, R.M., Krispin, O. & Lorey, F. (1993). Effects of domestic violence on children's behavior problems and depression. *Developmental Psychology*, 29(1), 44-52.

Stiles, M. (2002). Witnessing domestic violence: The effect on children. *American Family Physician*, 66(11), 2052-2067.

Stocker, C.M. & Youngblade, L. (1999). Marital conflict and parental hostility: Links with children's sibling and peer relationships. *Journal of Family Psychology*, 13(4), 598-609.

Sturge-Apple, M., Davies, P.T. & Cummings, E.M. (2006). Hostility and withdrawal in marital conflict: Effects on parental emotional unavailability and inconsistent discipline. *Journal of Family Psychology,* 20(2) 227-238.

Sturge-Apple, M., Davies, P.T., Winter, M.A., Cummings, E.M. & Schermerhorn, A.C. (2008). Interparental conflict and children's school performance: The explanatory role of children's internal representations of interparental and parent–child relationships. *Developmental Psychology*, 44(6), 1678-1690.

Stutzman, S.V., Bean, R.A., Miller, R.B., Day, R.D., Feinauer, L.L., Porter, C.L. & Moore, A. (2011). Marital conflict and adolescent outcomes: A cross-ethnic group comparison of Latino and European American youth. *Children and Youth Services Review*, 33(5), 663-668.

Taylor, P.J., Russ-Eft. D.F. & Chan, D.W. (2005). A meta-analytic review of behavior modeling training. *Journal of Applied Psychology*, 90, 692-709.

The Children's Society (2009). *A Good Childhood: Searching for Values in a Competitive Age*. London: Penguin.

Troxel, W.M. & Matthews, K.A. (2004). Review: What are the costs of marital conflict and dissolution to children's physical health? *Clinical Child and Family Psychology*, 7(1), 29-57.

Tschann, J.M., Flores, E., Pasch, L. & Marin, B.V. (1999). Assessing interparental conflict: reports of parents and adolescents in European and Mexican American families. *Journal of Marriage and the Family*, 61(2), 269-283.

Twenge, J.M., Campbell, W.K. & Foster, C.A. (2003). Parenthood and marital satisfaction: A meta-analytic review. *Journal of Marriage and Family*, 65(3), 574–583.

Van Goozen, S., Fairchild, G. & Harold, G.T. (2008). The role of neurobiological deficits in childhood antisocial behavior. *Current Directions in Psychological Science, 17*(3), 224-228.

Van Goozen, S., Fairchild, G., Snoek, H. & Harold, G.T. (2007). The evidence for a neurobiological model of childhood antisocial behavior. *Psychological Bulletin,* 133(1), 149-182

Volling, B.L. & Belsky, J. (1991). Multiple determinants of father involvement during infancy in dual-earner and single-earner families. *Journal of Marriage and the Family*, 53(2), 461-474.

Wadsworth, M. E. & Markman, H. J. (2012). Where's the action? Understanding what works and why in Relationship Education. *Behavior Therapy, 43*, 99-112.

Wasserstein, S.B. & La-Greca, A.M. (1996). Can peer support buffer against behavioural consequences of parental discord? *Journal of Clinical Child Psychology*, 25(2), 177-182.

Webster-Stratton, C. (1994). Advancing videotape parent training: A comparison study. *Journal of Consulting and Clinical Psychology*, 62(3), 583-593.

Webster-Stratton, C. & Hammond, M. (1998). Conduct problems and level of social competence in Head Start children: Prevalence, pervasiveness and associated risk factors. *Clinical Child Psychology and Family Psychology Review*, 1(2), 101-124.

Webster-Stratton, C. & Hammond, M. (1999). Marital conflict management skills, parenting style, and early-onset conduct problems: Processes and pathways. *Journal of Child Psychology and Psychiatry*, 40, 917–927.

Webster-Stratton, C. & Reid, M.J. (2003). The incredible years, parent, teacher and child intervention: Targeting multiple areas of risk for a young child with pervasive conduct problems using a flexible, manualized treatment program. *Cognitive and Behavioral Practice*, 8(4), 377-386.

Wetzler, S., Frame, L. & Litzinger, S. (2011). Marriage education for clinicians. *American Journal of Psychotherapy*, 65(4), 311-336.

Whiteside-Mansell, L., Bradley, R.H., Casey, P.H., Fussell, J.J. & Conners-Burrow, N.A. (2009). Triple risk: Do difficult temperament and family conflict increase the likelihood of behavioral maladjustment in children born low birth weight and preterm? *Journal of Pediatric Psychology*, 34(4), 396–405.

Whitson, S. & El-Sheikh, M. (2003). Moderators of family conflict and children's adjustment and health. *Journal of Emotional Abuse*, 3(1-2).

Wilson, B. & Stuchbury, R. (2010). Do partnerships last? Comparing marriage and cohabitation using longitudinal census data. *Population Trends*, 139, Spring 2010: Office for National Statistics.

Winter, M.A., Davies, P.T., Hightower, A.D. & Meyer, S. (2006). Relations among family adversity, caregiver communications, and children's family representations. *Journal of Family Psychology*, 20 (2), 348-351.

Wolchik, S.A., West, S.G., Sandler, I.N., Tein, J., Coatsworth, D., Lengua, L., Weiss, L., Anderson, E.R., Greene, S.M. & Griffin, W.A. (2000). An experimental evaluation of theory-based mother and mother-child programs for children of divorce. *Journal of Consulting and Clinical Psychology*, 68(5), 843-856.

Index

Page numbers in *italics* refer to tables.